From Teddy Tail Collars
to Itchy Tights

From Teddy Tail Collars to Itchy Tights

The History of Hereford Cathedral Junior School
(formerly the Cathedral Preparatory School)

by
Jill Howard-Jones

Logaston Press

LOGASTON PRESS
Little Logaston Woonton Almeley
Herefordshire HR3 6QH

First published by Logaston Press 1998
Copyright © Jill Howard-Jones 1998

ISBN 1 873827 15 6

Set in Times 11/13 pt by Logaston Press
and printed in Great Britain by
The Cromwell Press, Trowbridge

*For the pupils and staff of
Hereford Cathedral Junior School,
past, present, and future.*

Contents

Acknowledgements

I am grateful to the many past pupils and to past and present staff of Hereford Cathedral Junior School who have generously shared their memories for the benefit of this book.

In particular I wish to record my thanks to Hilary Alcock, the Rev. Canon David Apivor, Ray Boddington, Brian Bolt, Basil Butcher, Michael Carr, John Chadd, A.J. Christmas, Tim Compton, Ruth Dickson, Andrew Dodson, Fiona Field, Peter Griffiths, Bob Hall, John Hardwicke, Nigel Heins, Jennifer Higham, Keith and Judy Hill, Shirley Hurst, Father Andrew Hutchinson, D.E.N.B. Jones, Christopher Mann, William Quan, Stephen Sides, Hugh Thomas, Nora Thomas and daughters Deborah and Julia, the late P.S. Thompson, Jim Thorne, the Rev. Felix Watkins and John and George Warley.

I am also indebted to the following individuals and institutions in aiding my research: Bob Adams, Development Director of Hereford Cathedral School, Military Historian Major Martin Everett, Eve Finney of Churchill Gardens' Museum, Tim Lowe Headmaster of H.C.J.S., the *Hereford Times*, the Hereford County Library, the Cathedral Library, Ron Shoesmith and the Hereford Archaeological Unit (now Archaeological Investigations Ltd.), Brian Byron for the map, the Royal Navy Submarine Museum at Gosport for the photograph of the crew of D2, the National Monuments' Record Centre, the Hereford office of the Department of National Heritage, Cathedral Organist and Choirmaster Dr Roy Massey M.B.E. and the Dean and Chapter of Hereford Cathedral.

As always my thanks to my husband Ray for his support and dedicated proof-reading, Tony Bolton for his excellent photographs and to Andy Johnson for his efficiency in organising the publication of this book in time for the School's centenary.

Introduction

Before Tim Lowe arrived in Hereford to take up his appointment as Headmaster of Hereford Cathedral Junior School, someone sent him a copy of my book *Secret Hereford*. This led him to ask me to write a history of the school to celebrate its centenary in 1998: to provide both a record of the years and a 'good read'.

I have not written it! The many past pupils and staff who responded to my request for memories of 'the Prep' are the real authors of this book. My task has been to complete the jigsaw, to select and fit their personal recollections into the century's framework so that each decade of the School's history is seen through the eyes of those who were, or are there.

I have been entertained by their stories. I hope the reader will be too and join with me in congratulating Hereford Cathedral Junior School on its first hundred years!

Jill Howard-Jones,
March 1998.

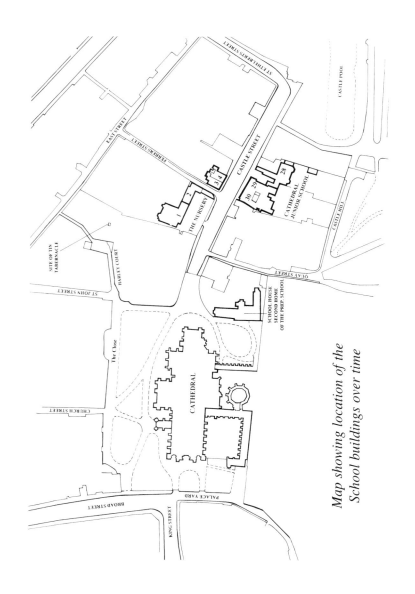

*Map showing location of the
School buildings over time*

CHAPTER 1

The Tin Tabernacle

The Cathedral Preparatory School was born in 1898 in an iron shed in the garden of Harley Court, the large old house standing in stately isolation at the end of a small lane behind the Dean's House (now the Old Deanery).

The then Headmaster of the Cathedral School, the Reverend Prebendary Murray Ragg, with an eye to extra income, saw the need to keep the Senior School fed with boarders and day pupils. He could now also assure parents that he was able to provide education for younger brothers. They would be taught by a schoolmistress (a spinster, of course).

Miss Dance was duly employed, promoted in due course to Headmistress and given an assistant, Miss Thompson. These two women ruled supreme over the garden schoolroom which became known as 'the tin tabernacle'. The first pupil was Allen Watkins, the only son of Alfred Watkins the antiquarian and photographer, who entered on 9th May 1898—something he boasted about throughout his life according to his own son, Felix.

The boys were strictly disciplined and gave the Dean who lived next door no cause for complaint. This was as well since a former Dean had had a difficult time with his neighbour—a certain Mistress Lincoln of Harley Court had once had an unrestricted view of the Deanery grounds from one of her windows which caused angry exchanges between herself and the Dean (whether over what the Dean saw or what the lady saw is unclear). Her

1

letter to him showed the strength of her feelings: 'We have often heard of "the Devil overlooking Lincoln"; in this case it is "Lincoln overlooking the Devil".'

At the beginning of the century, however, Mr Sharpley lived in Harley Court. Mr Sharpley was the Senior Master of the Cathedral School and knew better than to quarrel with the Dean. He was also *in loco parentis* acting as Housemaster to about twelve Prep school boarders whose daily education was catered for by Miss Dance in 'the Tin Tabernacle'.

The boarders came from a wide area. In 1908 two brothers arrived from a farm in Basingstoke, together with P.S. Thompson whose reminiscences have preserved for posterity glimpses of those early days. He remembers others from Skipton in Yorkshire, Wormleighton in Warwickshire, Llangunllo in Radnorshire, Timperley in Cheshire, and Castlemorton in Worcestershire. All would have been greeted by Mr Sharpley, an impressive dignified figure who was a strict disciplinarian.

P.S. Thompson, a vicar's son, recalls his arrival at Harley Court on 23 September 1908 on his ninth birthday. A long-standing friendship between his parents and the family of Mrs Sharpley was the reason for his parents taking him all the way from his father's parish of Eastleigh, a railway town in Hampshire between Winchester and Southampton, to boarding school in distant Hereford.

He describes the Preparatory School as being 'immediately behind Harley Court. It was a large room with wooden walls surrounded by green corrugated iron with large windows on the east side looking onto the playground, which was reached by a small passage-way at the far end, where coats and personal impedimenta were kept. At the same end of the room there was a small dais with a table and beside it a cupboard for books and stationery and other materials necessary for our education. The room itself was filled with desks from front to rear, lessons being held simultaneously at either end under the direction of the Headmistress, Miss Dance, and her assistant, Miss Thompson.' (How they divided their time between the classes he could not recall). 'At the back of the room was a covered passage which connected it with the small room where the boarders at Harley Court spent their leisure and had their meals.'

2

TERMINAL REPORT.

PREPARATORY DEPARTMENT.   *Xmas Term, 19.08*

Name *Thompson*   Class *II*   Average age of Class *9 yrs 5 mo*
                                        (9 boys)

 Position by Term's marks   *3*
 Position by Examination   *4*
 Position (final)   *4*

Subject:	Remarks.	
LATIN	*Good. shows great interest & intelligence*	*E. D*
HISTORY	*Very fair.*	*E. J.*
GEOGRAPHY	*Good.*	*E. J.*
WRITING	*Improved.*	*E. D.*
SPELLING	*Uncertain*	*E. J*
ARITHMETIC	*Good - has made great progress*	*E. D.*
SCRIPTURE	*Good.*	*E. D.*

Conduct: *Good -*   *E. D.*

Headmaster's Remarks on Examination: *A good start*

Next Term begins *Sat.ʸ Jan: 23ʳᵈ* Boys are expected to be in their places at 9.15 that morning.
Boarders return on Friday Jan. 22ᵗʰ W. H. MURRAY RAGG, M.A., *Headmaster.*

P.S. Thompson's Terminal Report, Christmas 1908

Miss Dance appeared to the small boy of nine as an 'elderly bespectacled woman.' He was uncertain of her age but knew that 'she was extremely fierce and frightened the life out of me. Her standards were very high and she never let you go till you had satisfied her requirements.'

Her efforts were rewarded for P.S. Thompson, who eventually became Headmaster of Bloxham, confessed that 'I learnt more from her in the two years I was at the Prep than from any master subsequently in double the time. Miss Thompson got similar

3

results by less rigid and spectacular means, being much younger than Miss Dance and possessing a more equable temperament.'

Their pupils' results were published every Christmas in the School List. In 1908, when there were 23 pupils in the school, P.S. Thompson came 4th out of 9 in Form 2, scoring 800 in Term and 890 in Exam—an impressive total of 1,690 out of a possible 2,000. His exercise books are so meticulously neat and careful, his copperplate writing such a pleasure to the eye that one wonders how three others could have excelled him.

Emphasis was placed on memory tests. These were frequently employed in Miss Dance's Geography lessons when pupils memorised counties and their capital towns and the whereabouts of rivers, bays, islands and hills with the aid of Longmans' Pictorial Geographical Readers. Geography also featured in handwriting lessons when pupils copied such revelations as 'England is divided into forty counties', 'Flamborough Head, a cape in Yorkshire' and 'Swansea Bay, south of Glamorganshire' into the 'Copy' books of the day.

Arithmetic involved addition, subtraction, multiplication and impressively long division. These skills were applied to square miles, yards, feet and inches, tons, hundredweights, quarters, pounds and ounces, and pounds, shillings and pence. They also managed small problems which reflected their agricultural environment.

I buy 1 pig at 11s. 6d.
I buy 10 pigs at (11/6 x 10) = £5 15s. 0d.
I sell 1 pig at 13s. 4d.
I sell 7 pigs (13/4 x 7) = £4 13s. 4d.
I lose (£5 15s. - £4 13s. 4d.) = £1 1s. 8d.

Budgeting and saving money were ideas implicit in problems set. One hundred pounds would have seemed an enormous sum to a small boy at the beginning of the century.

I have £100
In one month I spend £6 4s. 2d.
In 12 months (1 year) I spend (£6 4s. 2d. x 12) = £74 10s. 0d.
In 12 months (1 year) I save (£100 - £74 10s.) = £25 10s.

P.S. Thompson quickly mastered the present, future and imperfect tenses of first conjugation verbs in Latin. He observed, in the sexist attitude of the time that 'the girl does not plough' and was prepared to 'let the queen sing'! By the end of his second exercise book, he had graduated to such weighty comments as 'The slaves' great burdens will frighten the husbandmen' and 'You and the sailors have destroyed the soldiers' great works'!

Some English history was covered; P.S. Thompson wrote about Wat Tyler and the Peasants' Revolt.

Essentially, a classical education was the remit of the day, with Miss Dance aiming to please the Headmaster of the senior school, himself a classical scholar with a first class degree from Jesus College, Cambridge.

As was customary in public schools of that era, creativity was put on hold. No English essays or art work appear in the wealth of material bequeathed by P.S. Thompson.

English Literature, however, was not neglected. Mr Sharpley, another classical scholar, was nonetheless a lover of English Literature. On Sunday evenings in winter, he would invite his boarders to lie on the rug in his sitting room while he read to them. There, in the flickering firelight, they were transported to the highlands of Scotland to hear Roderick's bugle-horn as Mr Sharpley read of Scott's *Last Minstrel*. On another occasion they were treated to Matthew Arnold's poems, although how much they understood is debatable. *A Christmas Carol* must surely have conjured Marley's ghost from the shadows of the firelit sitting room to follow the boys upstairs to their dormitory.

The moral of Scrooge's experience was unlikely to be lost, but certainly not discussed. 'The days of easy understanding and mutual trust', says P.S. Thompson, 'had yet to come'. The teaching of religion remained strictly formal and conducted by Mrs Sharpley who examined pupils on their knowledge of the Collect for the week and the Church Catechism. P.S. Thompson describes the Sunday morning service in the Cathedral as 'the outstanding recollection' of his Prep school days. It followed a compulsory two hour walk to Dinedor, the apple orchards, or the Lugg meadows.

'At 10.50 a.m. we marched in pairs in our Eton suits to the north porch, where we stood in a long line till Mr Sharpley arrived to lead us in. We sat in the middle of the nave on the north side as members of a large congregation. At the end of Matins proper, Minor Canon Glennie and Minor Canon Duncombe processed from the chancel to the double prayer desk below the chancel steps to intone the Litany, the former taking the first part, the latter the second. After the anthem we were treated to a learned sermon of from 34-40 minutes from one of the Canons Residentiary. Normally we came out at ten minutes to one, more than ready for our Sunday lunch. It is the meal I have enjoyed most ever since! As a means of improving the shining hour—and 50 minutes, I used to have a private competition each term during favourable moments in the service reading the Prayer Book from the beginning, lesson tables and all, to see how far I could get by the end of term. I think I once got as far as the psalms! Sometime during Sunday afternoon, whether before or after the compulsory walk I cannot remember, we had Sunday School in the south transept, taken by Minor Canon Glennie under the eagle eye of Mrs Sharpley. In spite of this series of seemingly indigestible meals of religion, I never heard any complaint or antagonism. Without being cowed, we accepted things as they came and got on with them.'

As with his pupils, so with Mr Sharpley. Headmaster Murray Ragg's retirement was imminent and for whatever reason Mr Sharpley was not to be his successor. Inevitably therefore, he looked for a headship elsewhere. The stability of the Prep seems to have been threatened. P.S. Thompson records numbers varying a great deal, being as low as 11 in January 1911, when the three forms were reduced to two.

In 1912, the Headmaster, Prebendary William Henry Murray Ragg, 'retired' to a parish and pursued what one can assume was a more leisurely existence as Vicar of Tenbury until 1922, while maintaining his links with Hereford Cathedral as Prebendary of Bullinghope.

He was succeeded by Mr Henson in 1913 and at that time there were only 9 day boys and 5 boarders at the Prep School. Mr Sharpley duly left to become Headmaster of Louth School in Lincolnshire and Harley Court reverted to becoming a private residence.

The 'Tin Tabernacle' was eventually removed to the garden of the Headmaster's newly acquired Castle Street House, and relegated to a playroom for Prep school boarders who were accommodated in the Headmaster's House.

CHAPTER 2

Boy's Own Heroes

Like P.S. Thompson, and no doubt in common with several other classmates, Francis Eckley Oakeley was a vicar's son. Unlike P.S.T., however, Francis was a local boy and almost certainly not a boarder. His father was the Reverend James Oakeley of Holy Trinity, Whitecross, Hereford. One can imagine him walking to school along the Whitecross Road, past the Herefordshire & South Wales Eye and Ear Institution in Eign Street to Eign Gate, across Broad Street, down East Street and through the back gate of Mr Sharpley's house for registration with Miss Dance in the 'Tin Tabernacle'.

Being a fifth son, he was unlikely to have been spoilt though the stipend of 19th century clergy was generous by today's standards. No doubt his father would have required him to work hard to enter the professional avenues of the day for gentlemen's sons: the Church, the Army or the Navy.

Whilst at the Prep, Francis would have had no choice about working hard under the strict Miss Dance. What is clear is that he must have played hard too, especially when he entered the Senior School and had the opportunity of Rugby. He was to become an international Rugby player—every schoolboy's hero.

His skill on the Rugby field would have recommended him to the Navy. Perhaps academically he was less proficient, as he attended what appears to have been a 'crammer' (Eastman's) to enable him to pass the entrance exam to Osborne, the College for Naval Cadets on the Isle of Wight.

On hearing of his success in the exam, he would have had to be fitted for his uniform. This would have been supplied by Gieves, the naval outfitters in Savile Row, and consisted of tailor-made blue trousers and jacket with brass buttons and white collar tabs, topped with a naval cap.

Thus attired, he would have passed beneath Osborne's motto, emblazoned in large brass letters on the central oak crossbeam in the main hall, 'There is Nothing the Navy Cannot Do'.

Discipline at Osborne was strict. At 6 a.m. in summer and 6.30 in winter, the boys were woken by a bugler playing reveille. Francis would then have leapt out of bed, disturbing the rug of rough blue wool embroidered with his initials F.E.O. lying neatly at the end of his bed in the dormitory he shared with 30 others. At the first stroke of the cadet captain's gong, he'd kneel down and say his prayers. At two strokes of the gong he brushed his teeth and at three, jumped with the others into the green-tiled, cold-water plunge pool at the end of the dormitory.

Everything at Osborne was done at the double: the cadets were expected to run everywhere. Food was very unappealing, the boys spending their one shilling a week pocket money in the canteen hut on the playing fields where a naval pensioner sold fruit, stuffed dates and sweets.

The lack of privacy at Osborne was sorely felt by the then Prince of Wales who followed Francis there a couple of years later. He complained that the sixty or so cadets were 'never quiet from the time they get up till the time they go to bed'—a contrast to Holy Trinity Vicarage!

Francis must surely have excelled at Physical Training, taking bean-bag team games and daily Swedish drill in his stride. Compulsory games must have been a welcome diversion from Maths, Navigation, Science and Engineering, although the practical side of the engineering course involved visiting workshops on the River Medina and turns taken crewing a small steamer called *Beta*.

Royal Naval College, Dartmouth, followed Osborne as day followed night. Francis would have found the discipline a little less harsh despite the relentless tempo of life—only 3 minutes to undress in the evening. The cadets were more mature and burdens were easier to bear. As for Francis, he was already acknowledged as a sportsman of note. He won the cadet fencing competition Sabre v. Sabre at the Royal Naval and Military Tournament in 1906, and the first prize cadet competition, Foil v. Foil, in the following year. His remarkable skill as a Rugby player was also becoming widely known.

He passed out from Dartmouth on 15 Sept 1908—and while still only a Midshipman, began playing for the Services First Twenty. He was said to have good physique and was considered a first-rate half-back at Rugby.

On 15 March 1913, he played for England against Scotland at Twickenham. England, inspired by a fast and skilful set of forwards, won their first Grand Slam with a win by a single try in front of the Prince of Wales and 25,000 spectators. Nevertheless Francis Oakeley must have been disappointed because his English backs squandered chances with indifferent and unimaginative play, the press describing the English threequarter play as 'variable as an English summer'.

When England faced Wales at Twickenham on 17 January 1914, Oakeley was not included in the team. He had by then completed his submarine training and had been assigned to

England (v Scotland), 1913.
F.E. Oakeley is seated on the ground on the left

9

submarine C7. However, after Wales was defeated at Twickenham, most unluckily, by a single point, Francis was recalled for the match against Ireland on 14 February. Oakeley and Davies (Royal Navy & also recalled) set the centres on a move which resulted in a try in the corner. Davies scored another brilliant individualist's try near the posts which was converted, and a third try in the corner took the tally to 17-7. England were home and dry. The King was there to see it, on his first visit to Twickenham since his succession in 1910, and Asquith, the Prime Minister, was also among the 40,000 spectators.

Only five weeks later, on March 21, England played their last match on British soil before the start of the Great War. A spectator recorded that 'Few among us could have imagined that in six months' time, sport would be thrust out of our mind for five full years and that no less than eleven of the men who played in this splendid encounter would fall in the war.' Francis Oakeley was to be one of them. He had only seven months to live.

This match at Inverleith was deservedly memorable; some classic rugby was played that day. England gave the crowd a fine exhibition of open, attacking Rugby and seemed to be safely ahead half-way through the second spell when a remarkable Scottish recovery added to a thrilling afternoon. Despite a furious start from the Scottish forwards after the break, England answered the pleas and shouts of their supporters with three cracking tries. The result: England held on to win the Championship and Triple Crown for a second successive season.

Three weeks later, Francis Oakeley again played for England, this time against France at Stade Colombes, Paris, on 13 April. He was commended in the press for 'getting his backs moving for Poulton to score his fourth try. Greenwood converted each of these tries to raise England's points total to 39 and his own contribution to six conversions.' Unfortunately 'unsavoury scenes' on and off the field occurred during the second half as 'the English began to play attractive open Rugby which was contrary to the traditions of the French. Happily England was unruffled by these incidents.' Another English victory was secured and the skilful play of F.E. Oakeley (Royal Navy and United Services) had once again received public acclaim. The press were certainly in no doubt: Oakeley was the most promising player of the United Services.

His naval career had taken off too. By 1913, he had become Lieutenant Oakeley after gaining experience of serving in Battle & Cruiser Squadrons. It was, presumably recognition of his proficiency and potential that led to his being moved to H.M.S. Dolphin, the Portsmouth Submarine Depot, for the first five months of 1913 for instruction in underwater warfare. One can appreciate his excitement and fascination with the idea of submarine navigation 'visiting coasts of the world invisibly' as envisaged as long ago as the 17th century. Yet in the early 20th century submarines were still in their infancy and many hazards unrecognised. In 1904, the first A class submarine was 'run over' by a liner in the Solent. Undeterred, the Navy began to work its way through the alphabet, each letter signifying a new class of submarine larger and usually better than the last. Lt. Oakeley served first on C7. Whilst the B & C classes were coastal submarines, the D1 of 1914 was ocean-going and had diesel engines for surface propulsion. To the young lieutenant his transfer to D2 must have seemed a technical miracle, especially as in 1914, no navy could detect a submerged submarine, unless it had surfaced at the wrong moment, fired a torpedo or shown its periscope—even then it would have to be near enough to the surface to be rammed or hit by gunfire (no easy matter when the target was so small).

The Captain and his lieutenants knew too that in a submarine they had more opportunity to distinguish themselves since submarines frequently sailed alone or in small packs. They were surely better off than 'those unfortunate fellows in the trenches.'

Time for such comparisons was short since Oakeley was plunged into war. Within a year of his initial training on submarines he found himself serving on D2 under the command of 31 year old Lieutenant-Commander A.G. Jameson. On 23 November 1914, Submarine D2 was on patrol in the North Sea when a wave washed Jameson overboard. Lt. Oakeley heard the shout and as second-in-command, dashed to the conning-tower to take over. The submarine swung around, the men leaning over the conning-tower coaming to stare out through the gale force wind and rain for their captain. It was hopeless. They knew it was

D2 Crew September 1914, probably on return from patrol.
Officers seated in Row 2. From left to right Lt. F.E. Oakeley,
Lt. Cdr. Jameson and Lt. Copplestone.
(Courtesy of the RN Submarine Museum, Gosport)

impossible for anyone to survive in those wild seas, but Oakeley continued the search for two hours before calling it off. He eventually brought the submarine back to Harwich, where he faced the unenviable task of reporting Jameson's loss to his Flotilla Commander on H.M.S. Maidstone.

Oakeley was given no time to recover from this traumatic experience. The very next day, he left Harwich for another patrol in D2, now under the command of her new captain, 29 year old Lieutenant-Commander Clement Head. As the sub glided slowly past H.M.S. Maidstone, Lt. Cdr. Head raised his hand in salute. D2 was never to be seen again. She vanished somewhere in the North Sea, taking her new captain and his second-in-command to a watery grave with the rest of her crew. No evidence has ever been found to indicate her fate. Had the cruel sea, thwarted by its solitary victim a few days earlier, avenged itself on the whole crew? Or had D2 encountered a German torpedo boat?

Listed as killed in action, in only the 4th month of the war, at 23 years of age, Lieutenant Francis Oakeley was an acclaimed international Rugby star and war hero.

'The waters were his winding sheet, the sea was made his tomb; Yet for his fame the ocean sea, was not sufficient room.'

Francis Oakeley is typical of that lost heroic generation who gave their lives in the Great War. And his death remains mysterious.

Of the four young heroes commemorated in the House names of Hereford Cathedral Junior School (H.C.J.S.), which the preparatory school was later to become, Lieutenant Oakeley was the only one lost at sea. The story of Arthur Herbert Britten, however, is equally poignant but might require a stronger stomach in its reader!

He was born at his home at Edenhurst in Bodenham Road, Hereford, on 27 September 1893, the last of eleven children. His father, land agent William Edward Britten, was then 44 and his mother, Alice, 43. Notwithstanding the demands of their large young family, the parents had Arthur baptised within 4 weeks of his birth.

William only lived to see Arthur into the Cathedral Preparatory School in the wake of his brothers, while Alice survived to mourn both her youngest and her eldest sons.

Seventeen years separated the oldest and youngest brothers. To Arthur, Charles must have seemed a heroic figure. Locally too, he was esteemed in sporting circles; his career at the National Provincial Bank lasting only until a taste for action and adventure drove him into the Shropshire Yeomanry where he intrepidly survived the whole of the South African War. When world war broke out in 1914, he was in Johannesburg and immediately volunteered for service with General Botha against the Germans in South Africa.

Meanwhile young Arthur, having completed his education, likewise entered a bank, the Metropolitan, which he left only 6 months later in order to join another older brother then in business in Hereford. Aware of his country's need and his brother's apparent ease in bearing a charmed life while serving abroad, Arthur enlisted as a private in the Grenadier Guards.

That splendid regiment spent the winter of 1914 with gigantic trench rats for company, fat from feeding on the dead bodies in No Man's Land. How often, during the interminable waiting for enemy action, did Arthur fight sleep, willing warmth into his mud-soaked limbs, by dreaming of cricket at the Prep on the Castle Green?

The frost-bite won; blood poisoning intervened. Whale oil applied to his toes failed to prevent trench feet. Dreams of Hereford became reality: he was sent home; the price: amputation of several toes.

Recognition awaited him, however. Private Arthur Herbert Britten was awarded a commission—in the Gloucestershire Regiment, with whose 12th Battalion he was to serve continuously through the campaign of 1916-17. Thus the younger brother rose to the rank of lieutenant at almost the same time as the elder, since Charles, a gunner in the Cape Artillery had seen the completion of the war in South Africa and returned to England where he also obtained a commission, in the Royal Field Artillery. All seemed set fair.

Then, on 25 July 1916, Charles received shrapnel wounds in his chest and thighs. The poisonous nature of his injuries meant that both his legs had to be amputated.

> Does it matter—losing your legs?
> For people will always be kind
> And you need not show that you mind
> When others come in after hunting
> To gobble their muffins and eggs.
> *From* Does it Matter *by Siegfried Sassoon*

Perhaps mercifully, Charles didn't have to face his hunting pals at home again. He died in Abbeville Hospital in France; he was 40 years old. His obituary included a reference to his younger brother who had lost his toes in similar but less fatal circumstances and who 'has latterly been on home service but is again ordered abroad.'

That order took Lieutenant Arthur Britten to Belgium where, according to the Commonwealth War Graves Commission, he was killed on 14 April 1918, the *Hereford Times* for April 27th 1918 reporting that he was 'killed in action in France.' He has no known grave and so is commemorated with other members of the Gloucestershire Regiment on Panels 72-75 of the Tyne Cot Memorial to the Missing, 9 km north-east of Ypres in Belgium.

To his widowed mother, Alice, he left £223 10s. 11d. and his Military Cross won for 'conspicuous bravery and devotion to duty' at the taking of Messines Ridge.

His old school subsequently recognised his bravery too, giving his name to 'Britten' House. Lieutenant Woodhall and Captain Matthews also gave their names to Houses. All four are remembered for their distinguished service to their country but each had something more to offer than his commitment to the armed forces.

John Bredel Matthews, born in 1891, was first and foremost a talented young architect. He came second in all England in the Royal Institute of British Architecture exam before he enlisted. He served with the 3rd Battalion of the North Staffordshire Regiment and was attached to the 8th Battalion of the Leicestershire Regiment. Indeed it was while he was commanding his company in the Leicestershire Regiment that he won the Military Cross for 'conspicuous gallantry and devotion to duty'. The *London Gazette* for 16 August 1917 records the incident.

'At a critical moment during an attack, when it was held up by enemy wire and under intense machine gun barrage, he rallied his men with great coolness and withdrew them to shelter. The skill with which he handled his men under extreme adverse circumstances undoubtedly saved many lives. The fact that his company had been reserved for a counter-attack and that he had to alter his plans at a moment's notice in the attack, speaks volumes for the resource which he displayed at a critical moment.'

Seven weeks later, Captain Matthews was killed in action at Polygon Wood and subsequently commemorated with Lieutenant Britten and thousands of others at the Tyne Cot Memorial in Belgium, because he had no known grave.

At home, the Royal Institute of British Architecture, conscious of his outstanding promise as a young architect, requested that the

Mayor of Leicester publicly present Captain Matthew's parents with his Military Cross.

The fourth hero of the First World War and whose name graces Woodhall House was the youngest. Indeed John Woodhall's name is the only one to appear in the 1908 Hereford senior school list, by which time he had passed into the second form of the school and distinguished himself by coming 4th out of 21. His name doesn't appear in subsequent lists, since he left to attend West Heath School, Hampstead, and from there progressed to Ellesmere College, Shropshire, joining the O.T.C. in 1912.

By the age of 18, in August 1915, he was already a 2nd Lieutenant in the Oxford and Buckinghamshire Light Infantry, and was transferred to the Machine Gun Corps in January 1916 for service in France and Flanders.

The formation of the Machine Gun Corps was a late move on the part of the British. By that time the Germans had already become the experts in this field. Nevertheless, Lieutenant John Woodhall applied his considerable intelligence to this new initiative and won the Military Cross, the *London Gazette* of 26 September 1916 describing how 'He rushed a machine gun up to the crater of a newly exploded mine, and by his pluck and skill held the enemy off for 40 minutes until our raiding party had withdrawn. He and his team were under heavy fire.'

Although wounded, he recovered quickly and was posted to Egypt. He was not to return, meeting his death during the 3rd Battle of Gaza, while serving with 157 Company of the Machine Gun Corps on November 8th 1917, at Wadi Hesi in Palestine. He lies in the Gaza War Cemetery in Israel: Plot 19. Row A. Grave 13. He was barely 20 years old.

When House competes against House at H.C.J.S., the name of John Woodhall lives on, together with that of Francis Oakeley, Arthur Britten and John Matthews. Some small compensation, perhaps, for the supreme sacrifice each made?

CHAPTER 3

Enter Ma Gam

We left the 'Tin Tabernacle' relegated to a playroom in the Headmaster's garden, so where was the Prep school accommodated thereafter? We know that in 1912, a new headmistress, Miss Linda B. Gamlen, formerly private tutor to the Bulmer boys, was appointed and that by 1915, the Preparatory Department of Hereford Cathedral School was certainly situated in what local historian Basil Butcher describes as 'the long brick building facing the Cathedral'.

A.F. Stallard, whose mother had just been appointed as house surgeon to the County Hospital and whose father was a missionary, arrived in Hereford from India in 1915 and was despatched immediately to the Cathedral Prep, 'which was a bit bewildering after my companionship with a lot of little brown children. I was in the classroom on the ground floor facing the Cathedral's east end.' This was perhaps Miss Clay's room (Form 1), which Basil describes as 'next to the Vicars' Choral College'. Form 2 was with Miss Phillips in the room to the left of the main entrance. Miss Allen's class (Form 3) was in the room with the bay end, while Miss Gamlen and Form 4 were upstairs over Form 3.

Max Marriott supplies explicit directions to what would seem to have been the pupils' front door entrance to the Prep in 1919. 'Enter from Castle Street, bear left as you go into the Close, leaving the Lady Chapel on your right, then there is a door marked "Cathedral School", which was the entrance to the Prep School when I was a boy.'

*Miss Gamlen (in foreground in white hat) at Wyeside on
Sports' Day. Mr Howard Bulmer is in the background*

There was no room for the Headmistress to live on the
premises in what was later referred to as 'The Old Preparatory
Block' (then incorporated into the senior boarding 'School
House'), so Miss Gamlen lived on Aylestone Hill. Her staff also
resided nearby; Miss Phillips in Nelson Street, Miss Clay in
Bodenham Road and Miss Allen on Broomy Hill.

C.J. Christmas has fond memories of Miss Clay, a very kind gentle lady who was 'particularly good with the first form and did first aid when necessary.'

Miss Phillips, the daughter of Major Phillips whom her pupils understood to be a 'great' man, was of sterner stuff, even frightening, indicating that Form 2 was a very different world to Miss Clay's gentle regime. Basil tells how 'she confiscated my water pistol at the start of one term, saying I would get it back at the end of term—I never did, it could not be found! I held that against her for some time!'

There was also Miss Allen who played the piano at the morning 'service' which finished with a hymn. On their birthdays, the boys were allowed to choose their own hymn. Basil used this to advantage, choosing Onward Christian Soldiers, 'not because it meant anything to me, but because it had several long verses and so cut down lesson time!'

Mischiefmakers and swots alike looked up to Miss Gamlen, 'known as "Ma Gam" in the nicest possible way.' Basil describes her as 'a remarkable head, something special, strict but fair,' adding 'except on one occasion when she accused me of doing something which I denied. She boxed my ears in front of the assembled class; I can see her now, very red in the face. But it was not me. I took it, having the sense to realise there were a number of occasions when I had done something and had not been caught! In any case, had I complained at home, knowing me, Father would not have believed me and might have added his punishment!'

A.F. Stallard recalls that 'Miss Gamlen, although very pleasant on the whole, used a cane on the worst offenders: on the hand, of course!' His most vivid memory, however is associated with acute embarrassment as persistent recollections often are. Cries of 'Who killed the donkey?' in Form 1 required the response 'the man in the white hat'. 'Indeed', he admits, 'I had a white hat, and blushed deeply, now being nearly six years old.'

Basil Butcher doesn't remember 'much of what we were taught', either, 'but what did stick were manners and appearance. There were set rules for behaviour outside school in Castle Street, the Cathedral Close and the City Centre—no hands in pockets, jacket buttoned up, caps always on and raised to grown-ups we knew.' (I believe only the first of these still applies!) Strictly out of bounds was Greenlands' basement toy department with its displays of Hornby trains, Meccano and toy soldiers—unless accompanied by parents, Norlands' nannies or other approved folk.

Understandably school outings were viewed as highspots in the year, remaining in focus long after the daily routine had been lost in mist. This is reinforced in C.J. Christmas's diary for 1921 which contains no references to lessons except that on November 8th 'it was very snowy and there was school instead of football'! Sporting activities are assiduously recorded, including a football match at Tenbury in February, Prep School Sports and Big School Sports in March, numerous games of cricket—especially that marking Miss Gamlen's birthday on July 8th, followed by the Regatta on July 21st.

4th formers were granted the top class's privilege of regular outings. The popular Pond Trawling Trip was to Tupsley Brickworks, (the pond is now filled in), where they caught newts in a net with a long handle.

The annual trip to Bulmers has become an institution, although the factory was only in Ryeland Street when Miss Gamlen first took her pupils to be greeted by Howard Bulmer himself. Ten years later, Brian Bolt (1928-32) remembers the vats as 'vast, towering above', but in later years when he visited Bulmers in a professional capacity, 'the vats seemed to have shrunk'. Such are the perceptions of childhood!

Did the Cathedral Tower on 21st March 1921 seem higher then than to today's eleven year olds? Yesteryear's 4th form were also treated in November to a trip up All Saints' tower to see the chained library. Of the two outings, the former made more impact on Basil, who explains how it was carefully planned so that they arrived in the Belfry at 4 p.m. when the clock struck. 'We all had our fingers in our ears and took them out when the striking finished. No-one had told us of the Bidding bell at five past, which scared us to death!'

Such were the highlights of their last year at the Prep for 4th form boys who started Big School on the 17th January 1922— with abiding memories of Miss Gamlen, no doubt. For John

Miss Phillips and Miss Gamlen

Matthews (1918-22) it was the 'great rush to push Miss Gamlen's bike back to school' after football at Wyeside. 'Miss Gamlen was adored by all the boys in spite of the fact that she maintained firm discipline and was known to give half a dozen with the cane if necessary.'

That remarkable lady who could instil fear and inspire adoration simultaneously was to take the Cathedral Prep into its next significant phase.

CHAPTER 4

'Charming 28'

1925 marks a significant development in the history of the Prep, which must have been personally very gratifying to Miss Gamlen, for she acquired (through the auspices of the Headmaster and his Governors), No.28 Castle Street.

This magnificent white early Georgian house has features dating back to the 16th century, although the Royal Commission on Historical Monuments describes it as being 'almost entirely rebuilt in the 18th century' around the central walls enclosing the Hall and Staircase. The latter are lined with panelling dating from around 1700 but the dado to the Hall is even earlier (mid-17th century) moulded panelling with a top frieze of incised 'strap work' carving. The oldest part of the house appears to be the 16th century fireplace in the room south-east of the Hall. The horizontal piece with a running pattern of vine, foliage and fruit is early 16th century. The two end pieces are carved with double roses, probably bosses from a roof, while the side pieces have an unusual ornamental border with a repeating pattern of interwoven waving lines of late 16th century date.

The house is set well back from the street and seems to be following the trend as several other buildings in Castle Street are similarly positioned. On Taylor's 1757 map, the house is shown set back with a narrow access. By the time of Curley's plan, in 1858, the entry had been improved with a drive leading round a grass-covered area. By the early 20th century the grass had again disappeared.

*Sixteenth century fireplace, 28 Castle Street, with pupils
William Cass and Katherine Kempe. (Tony Bolton)*

In 1925, the top floor flat of No.28 was occupied by the Cathedral School Chaplain and his family. His son, the Reverend Canon David Apivor, recalls, 'From Castle Street, one entered the building through iron fencing and an area which I suppose was gravelled; certainly it was not any kind of garden. On the right side was a garage, where the Headmaster Dr Crees kept his car, though as an avid cyclist he rarely drove.'

The garage was one of the many attributes of a building which for many years had been a private house. According to Kelly's Register for 1905, it belonged to Henry Child Beddoe. This gentleman also appears in the 1885 Register under the Commercial Section as 'solicitor, proctor and notary public, sec. to Bishop of Hereford, steward to custos [guardians] and vicars and registrar of the diocese and county treas. Cathedral Close.' It would appear that he moved out of the Cathedral Close on retirement and settled at No.28. In Jakeman & Carter's Directory of 1914, the private residents of 28 are listed as the Misses Beddoe.

Fourteen years later, its use changed permanently from private house to school. Canon Apivor recalls the folk who lived either side. 'The Steels, in No.29, were nice people: he a typical English gentleman lawyer; their son, a tall young man, who I think was an Old Boy of H.C.S., and who eventually took over the practice. Mrs Steel, very deaf, talked very loudly. I don't think we had any social contact with them really. Some rather nice folk lived at No.30, a retired doctor, J.C. Dubuisson, and his sister, great churchgoers, of course, as everyone more or less had to be who lived round there.' (According to the 1937 directory, the Steels are in fact listed as having Nos.29 and 30, the former as their residence and the latter as their offices, with the Du Buissons listed at No.31)

But in No.28 was now ensconced the Hereford Cathedral School Preparatory School, for the first time a separate unit, while being an integral part of the Cathedral School and subject to its Headmaster and governors. The *Hereford Times* for Saturday, October 10th 1925, describes the auspicious opening of the new premises.

'HEREFORD CATHEDRAL SCHOOL PREPARATORY SCHOOL
Dr Crees, the principal and staff of the Preparatory School were At Home on Monday at the new School house which has been recently acquired (No 28 Castle Street). The At Home, which was held in the garden, was intended to inaugurate the work of the School, and there was a large attendance of parents and friends. Dr Crees, in welcoming the visitors, said that the present term marked a new epoch in the history of the Preparatory School. Owing to the increase of numbers in the Upper School it had been necessary for the Preparatory School to find fresh quarters, and he had been faced with a difficult problem. It had been possible however, to find a house adjacent to the Upper School buildings and the Boarding House, which had a dignity and charm of its own and a very pleasant garden. As regards numbers, they had increased considerably this term, and they had made an excellent start in every way. The Dean of Hereford (Chairman of the Governors of the Cathedral School), in a graceful speech congratulated Dr Crees on his recent marriage, and wished the Preparatory School all prosperity in its new venture. He explained under what circumstances it had been necessary for the Preparatory School to seek fresh quarters, and said that there was every reason to believe that in the charming house which had been acquired, the School would be as successful in the future as in the past. Miss Gamlen, the Headmistress of the Preparatory School, said that boys

between the ages of six and twelve were a very interesting psychological study. They needed to be taught to discriminate between good and evil, what was wise and unwise. At the Preparatory School they endeavoured to give the boys the community spirit. This was a very strong feature of the School's work. After tea the company inspected the house and the various classrooms, and the oak-panelled hall was much admired.'

In the same issue of the *Hereford Times*, a Mr Baker was reported as stating in connection with the recommended appointment at Scudamore's Girls' School of Mrs M.E. Wilson that 'no one had opposed the appointment of married women teachers more than he had, and he considered that in future it should be understood that women teachers should resign immediately on marrying.'

The commitment of 'spinsters' to the teaching profession is underlined by both Miss Gamlen's strict moral code and the fact that her long serving staff remained devoted to their duty and firmly unmarried. Their word was law to their pupils who dared not question their authority.

David Apivor recalls 'having the daylights frightened out of me during Assembly which was held in Form 1, in the classroom on the left of the hall, looking out to the garden, when Miss Gamlen in a rage brought down her cane on the desk where I was standing and jolly near struck my hand.' The reason? 'Two horrors' (his contemporaries) had put ice in the pillar box, which still stands in front of No.28.

His memories of the classroom on the right of the hall weren't very cheerful either! 'It was very dark, largely due to the enormous tree in No.29, house of lawyers A.D. Steel and his son Tom, and their offices. I have always understood that that was one of the reasons why I have had to wear glasses from about 6 years of age, as that classroom was such a strain on the eyes!'

Form 4, the senior form taught by Miss Gamlen, was also on the ground floor, situated on the left as you entered from the front door. Brian Bolt (1928-32) remembers it as a small room with individual hinged desks, two of which his father bought for Brian and brother Tom's bedrooms (to induce the prep habit), when the desks were updated in 1930. The 'secret' door in the wall on the right-hand side of the fireplace fascinated the boys. It was the width and height of a dummy bookcase full of 'leather-bound'

Scene from 'Alice in Wonderland' in 1931
with C. Humby as Alice, Ward Smith as Rabbit,
B. Williams as Dormouse and G. Pitt as Hatter

books, presumably the study when the building was a private house. The door led into a side entrance lobby, from which there was access to the front of the house and the garden. It was used as a cloakroom then and still is, apparently!

Likewise the door in the centre of the bottom garden walk which led into the roadway between Quay Street and the Castle Green will be familiar to many old boys, who welcomed its offer of escape from study to exercise on the Castle Green!

David Apivor also has vague memories of a downstairs flat on the right of the front hall, occupied by some people called Jenkins, 'caretakers and/or cleaners who had some kids, one of whom cried all the time.' Their flat looked out on an open, empty yard used for hanging washing. A perpetual war of nerves was waged between the Jenkins and David's mother over water. Use of it downstairs deprived the Apivors in the top flat of running water.

On the first floor, below the Apivors and above the Jenkins family, was the remaining classroom housing Form 3. Their teacher, Miss Roberts, a recent addition to the staff 'unlike Miss

Phillips and Miss Allen who had been there ages' was young, small and athletic and a favourite with the boys. 'Wordy' (J.C. Wordsworth, alleged nephew of the poet and Senior Classics Master at H.C.S.) also lived on the first floor, occupying the one (or two) rooms on the right. The 'strange snorting noises' he made in his bath intrigued young listeners!

The other occupant of the second floor was Miss Gamlen herself. Her flat included a living room and bedroom, the former looking out on to the garden above Form 2 and nearest to No.29. She could thus keep an eye on playground activities from her bay window.

The Apivors' top flat appears to have been more spacious since it housed the Chaplain, his wife and three boys. They were nonetheless grateful to eventually move to the Cloisters, 'to our best home in Hereford'.

Perhaps David Apivor's memories of school were more fun than living on the premises. He shares with John Matthews (1918-22) recollections of running down to Wyeside in football boots and the great rush, on the return, to gain the privilege of pushing Miss Gamlen's bike through the Close and back to school. When Miss Gamlen smiled approval, the sun shone but the 'grim face' of Headmaster Dr Crees remained unchanged. The big event prior to the arrival of the Apivors in 1925 was that 'Dr Crees had descended from his Olympian heights and married Miss Martin, who was the matron of the boarding part of H.C.S, mostly quartered in the Headmaster's house. To most people, this was the most unlikely thing he would ever do. She had always been referred to as "the Queen", a term he used too. For reasons which had various explanations, he was known as "Kink"; I doubt if anyone would have been brave enough to tell him that. What on earth would Dr Crees have said to GIRLS in the school, we literally risked expulsion by being seen talking to them.'

Unpopular as Dr Crees seemed to be with his pupils, both the Senior School and the Prep made substantial progress in the decade immediately after his appointment in 1920. J.C. Eales-White records that in 1919 the Preparatory School had 77 pupils, including boarders, and between 1920-30 always mustered at least 40-50 boys.

Significantly Eales-White in the *Record of Hereford Cathedral School* reserves this era's accolade for Miss Gamlen: 'It will at once be apparent that the value of the preparatory department as a feeder to the Cathedral School could hardly be overestimated, and the increasing prosperity of the latter is gratefully acknowledged as due in a large measure to the devoted preliminary work of Miss Gamlen and her colleagues.' The reputation of Miss Gamlen and her colleagues was such that it was felt necessary to stress in 3 consecutive announcements in the September 1925 editions of the *Hereford Times* 'upon the move of the premises that there has been no change of staff and the school will be conducted on the same lines as previously ... in its new and commodious premises at 28, Castle Street.'

The curriculum remained focused on the 3Rs, with subjects like History and Geography firmly relegated to second place.

Despite the move 'down the road', the link with the 'Big School' remained as strong as ever. In Form 4, the Prep School boys even wore the same uniform as the Upper School: striped long trousers, black 'bum-freezer' jackets, two inch wide white teddy tail collars stiffly starched, (Teddy Tail, the *Daily Mail* children's cartoon character wore such a collar), regulation black lace-up shoes, grey socks with blue and yellow bands on top. The school scarf and tie have barely changed but blue caps with half inch yellow ribbon sewn on in three horizontal bands were compulsory.

Occasionally they also attended a service in the cathedral's Lady Chapel in the company of the Upper School, while those Prep school boys who stayed to school lunch joined 40 Upper School boarders in a crowded hut at the back of No.1 Castle Street, then the Headmaster's House. Brian Bolt says the meat and two veg (fish on Friday) was nourishing but sadly lacking in flavour or finesse. Rice, tapioca, semolina or rolypoly pudding were regular dishes for 'afters'. If the first course was not completely eaten, pupils were denied the second. (No loss for Brian who detested milk puddings!)

Grace was said before meals usually by Miss Phillips and the Headmaster. 'His wife Mrs Crees, a woman of both stature and girth hovered around in a white coat in a supervising role putting the fear of God into us all. There was no joking, talking or fooling about.'

The trek to Wyeside for football and cricket on Tuesday and Thursday afternoons also continued. Miss Gamlen and Miss

Phillips on their 'sit up and beg' ladies cycles set a medium pace with Miss Gamlen leading and Miss Phillips bringing up the rear. Occasionally there was cross country along the river meadows. Then the boys were accompanied by sporty, 'good fun' Miss Copley, 'a jolly-hockey-playing lady suitably attired, coaxing us regardless of the weather.'

The Annual Summer Sports—100 yards; 200 yards; Relay Race; ½ mile; Egg and Spoon; 3 legged and Sack Race—is remembered as a grand occasion. Surely the sun always shone on mothers in fine dresses, hats and parasols displaying genteel mirth at their husbands disporting themselves in the fathers' race, before partaking of tea and fairy cakes under the pavilion verandah.

The weekly swimming lesson in the new Public Baths in Edgar Street, a prestigious building of its time, was also an occasion to be savoured. The boys had the bath to themselves for a two hour period on Wednesday afternoons. Their parents paid fees direct to the instructor who apparently had 100% success with pupils who recall picking up bricks from the 7 feet deep end and recovering pennies thrown in by spectating parents. Several mothers assisted with 'starters', while the more confident and venturesome dived from the top diving board, recalled by Basil Butcher as being 'about 12 feet, quite high in those early days of diving.' Despite the 'burning' sensation in the eyes from the heavily chlorinated water (no goggles then), these sessions were evidently enjoyed, as were the penny buns, hot from the oven from the baker's on the other side of town, with which appetites were assuaged before the journey home.

Miss Gamlen firmly dismissed any moans about 'burning eyes' in the interests of her pupils' survival in water. She wanted the best out of her boys. A much coveted award was the one she gave on Speech Day to the boy from the 4th form who had done the most to help in all ways: looking after younger ones in the playground, keeping paths swept, putting sweet papers in waste paper baskets. She was undoubtedly the mainspring of the school's ethos, declares Ray Boddington (1933-36), who recalls her energy and outstanding personality and tells of her concern when he was suffering from a preliminary attack of appendicitis. She administered brandy—which he considered worse than the complaint itself!

View of garden of 29 Castle Street from number 28.
(Tony Bolton)

Like Miss Gamlen, Miss Clay and Miss Phillips remained dedicated to their profession for over two decades. The former continued 'motherly' and gentle in appropriate kindergarten style like a mother hen with her chicks, while stern Miss Phillips moulded her charges into some sort of shape, controlling break in the playground (especially at conker time), policeman-style with a whistle. Her pupils remember her as a very upright, precise bespectacled lady with a bun. Her military bearing caused many pupils to associate her with her father, Major Phillips (known in his regiment as 'Chesty Phillips'). Indeed after the outbreak of war, she introduced her own unofficial cadet force, proudly marching her cadets round the square. 'The nearest I've seen to a female Sergeant Major', according to pupil John Warley, who in

1997, met a former teacher who served under Miss Phillips, and confided how that military lady had terrified her pupils. 'She put the fear of God into us too' was the reply! Hers was a stern image apparently unmitigated by humour.

Not so, Miss Gamlen. One of her favourite stories concerned the pupil, who when asked if he knew what he was going to do when he left school, said he was going into the Church and hoped to become a Bishop, for they enjoyed a fine lifestyle: They lived in large houses with chauffeur and gardener and didn't seem to do too much work! She added that this particular boy had indeed become a Bishop, but never mentioned his name!

Anyway she didn't have to, for the standing of 'the Prep' was plainly reflected in the achievement of its many old boys who held high offices in the Church, Services, Government and Colonial Departments, Medicine, Law and the Universities. Many of course were the sons of professionals, such as Ronald Francis (1933-6) whose mildly eccentric father was the doctor living in St. Ethelbert Street who continued well into the 1960s to be driven, bowler-hatted, by his serving-man in a pony and trap to visit his patients. Predictably, Ronald too became a doctor. For him as for many, the Prep was the first step taken on the road to fulfilling parental ambition in a chosen profession.

Understandably Miss Gamlen delighted in the achievements of her old boys and together with Miss Phillips threw an annual tea-party in the Booth Hall, Imperial Cafe or Green Dragon in their honour. During their time at school she had kept a note of all their birthdays in her 'bible' and recorded their upward progress which she measured regularly with a foot-rule in front of the whole school. She never forgot a boy's name despite the numbers that passed through. Her old boys showed their appreciation in turn by regular attendance at her tea parties, while Howard Bulmer presented her with a Morris 8 which Basil Butcher taught her to drive. She proved an excellent pupil. He put a match behind the wheel on a slope, and told her to start without crushing it. And she did! Out of appreciation for her lessons, she gave him 'the Bible to be read as literature' and wrote in it, 'From one teacher to another, who kept her on the straight (sometimes) and narrow path.' It was a path from which she never deviated in her time as Headmistress.

CHAPTER 5

Paying the Price

Even Miss Gamlen couldn't teach forever, although the spark of interest kindled by her Latin lessons remained to the end. Keith Hill (1940) remembers how 'we all cheered when the Romans won a victory in the Carthaginian wars and the battle was underlined in red chalk on the blackboard.'

She also continued to be '100% interested in everything her pupils did' declares John Warley. An incident related by John Chadd (1938-43) illustrates this well.

'In the early years of the war my father came home on leave from the army and brought me a model anti-aircraft gun which fired little silver shells. At the time I thought it was the most magnificent toy I had ever seen and next morning took it to school with great pride. Miss Gamlen was fascinated with it and fired it herself with great enthusiasm. I think the gun was made of cast-iron because it was quite heavy. Unfortunately someone dropped it on the floor and it broke into several pieces.

'Miss Gamlen seemed as distressed as I was and spent much of the day with a soldering iron attempting to repair the gun. It never fired again but she did get it back into one piece.'

Discipline too was still enforced in her own inimitable way. John Chadd tells of 'two particular boys quarrelling for several days. They were literally engaged in a running battle. And finally Miss Gamlen lost patience. She assembled all the form in their classroom and produced two pairs of boxing gloves and made the

34

Hereford Cathedral Preparatory School
Summer 1943

M. Smith J. Matthews P. Rogers B. Tummey E. Anstice J. Farr R. Jepps N. Farr B. Wright G. Downes E. Launder

J. Dent R. Jancey M. Slatford H. Hartland I. Bond K. Morris J. Rogers G. Bishop-Laggett A. Tringham W. Sockett D. Volpé C. Greenland G. Lough J. Ruscoe D. Ford

A. Francis B. Evans D. Gittins M. Perlman P. Richards P. Ferguson I. Hogg R. Hartley D. Wust K. Volpé M. Bauginet D. Miller P. Davies F. Bagnall G. Windsor-Lewis P. Pritchard R. Townsend M. Ford J. Edwards K. Wilson I. McIntyre R. Townley

J. Cotton J. Jones M. Allsebrook R. Atkins T. Moore J. Fellows G. Warley J. Warley M. Townley J. Chadd J. Woolfenden H. Yeomans

R. Gardiner P. King M. Harley Miss E.N. Janes G. Barnes Miss G.M. Phillips C. Morgan Miss L.B. Gamlen D. Wall Miss E.M. Clay R. Hiles Miss M.L. French B. Jones E. Bulmer J. Woods

M. Colley S. Adamson E. Bellgard D. Darlington G. Shepard S. Richards R. Owens R. Hathaway M. Bond G. Miller Y. Davies M. Simpson K. Jones A. Weston M. Walker J. Stephens D. Lowe J. Whittal F. Wheeldon J. Holloway

two offenders fight it out until they were nearly dropping or, as she said, had knocked the sense out of each other.'

This is similar to the story told me by the Warley twins whose perpetual fight with 'two bullies' was also resolved with boxing gloves in Miss Gamlen's study—perhaps another version of the same tale? Both serve to show that Miss Gamlen was scrupulously fair (though today both guns and boxing would be regarded as politically incorrect) and endorses George Warley's comment that 'her discipline always stood us in good stead.'

When she retired on July 28th 1943, the numbers of pupils entering the school each year indicated financial stability and public confidence. From 1931-1939, the average intake was 21 spread over the three terms. In 1940-1 it escalated to 38, when evacuation began to swell numbers. The yearly intake remained in the lower thirties till it rose dramatically to 51 in 1943 with a flood of evacuees including twins John and George Warley from Guernsey who have stayed in Hereford ever since.

By retiring at this juncture, Miss Gamlen was seen to be handing over a thriving school. 1943 also marked the end of 30 years' dedicated service.

For whatever reason, the chosen successor, Miss Emerson, resigned in July 1944, after only one year. Anthony Weston (1942-49) recalls how she 'endeared herself during her short period of office by discontinuing Saturday morning school.' Mr Thomas's efforts to revive it later were strongly opposed by the parents.

Although Gwendoline Phillips, Miss Gamlen's unofficial deputy since 1912, was not promoted on her friend's retirement, she did finally become Headmistress in September 1944. Sadly she had been in the wings too long understudying for her big part which came too late. Miss Clay (1918-43) who recognised the time had come for her own retirement, warned her colleague with these words, 'We're all getting older; nobody's indispensable.'

Once the school had been bought by Mr Thomas, who thus became Headmaster, she had to relinquish her role and it wasn't long before Mr Thomas was to bid Miss Phillips a final 'Good afternoon' as his widow succinctly put it. So ended 38 years' of dedicated service to the Prep.

Hereford Cathedral Preparatory

School Sports, 1942

Event *100 yards Open 9 years*

2nd *J. W. Warley*

1942 Sports Card for 100 yards' race awarded in lieu of a prize,
the value of which was donated to the Red Cross

The fact that the number of entrants dropped in 1944 to 18 (picking up again from 1945-7) must not be imputed to the reaction of parents to the appointment of the new Headmistress but was more likely signalling the end of the evacuation era.

Anthony Weston notes the effect that the War—albeit distant —had on himself and fellow pupils.

'Many fathers were conscript soldiers. There was the constant need for patriotic frugality. It was, to the grief of the teaching staff, not entirely practicable to maintain proper standards of gentlemanly conduct. We were not merely allowed but even encouraged, for reasons of food economy, to suck through our straws the very last drops of our bottled milk and to ignore the vulgarity of the resulting noise!

'However some semblances of pre-War civilisation remained. There was usually a small posse of nannies (some uniformed) outside the school gates awaiting the release of their young charges. I recall, moreover, one very individual distinction. At the end of War in Europe in 1945 we were formed into the shape of a 'VE' in the playground. I found myself at the end of the middle stroke of the 'E'. I proudly believed this to be a celebration of my personal contribution to the downfall of Naziism.'

Sportsmen George and John Warley remember their disappointment at the cutbacks necessitated by war time. First and second team colours were cut out to save expense and what would have been spent on them was given to the Red Cross. John's certificates won at Sports Day fill a scrap book: Sack Race, Tug of War, 100 Yards' Handicap, 200 Yards' Open under 10, Barrow Cup etc.

These were pupils' impressions but Miss Gamlen, Miss Phillips and Miss Clay had to face over 15 years of coming to terms with learning that those they had taught as little boys would never return from the war. Edward Bulmer, who entered the school as early as 1915 and later joined the R.A.F., was killed. John Hawksford Hinks (1918-1922) died on active service in Flanders in May 1940. George Bevan (1918-23) of R.A.F. Bomber Squadron, was reported missing on July 31st 1941, while Oscar Theodore Bulmer (1921-23) died in Belgium in 1944. The following also gave their lives:

> Noel Watkins (1921 -23)
> Alwyn David James (1923-26)
> Claude Slatter (1923-27)
> Patrick R.C. Fisher (1924-25)
> Richard Emerson Savage (1924-25)
> Roger Hereford James (1924-28)
> Christopher Averay Jones (1927-31)
> Basil Whitfield Drew (1928)
> Bevill Cyril Bowerman (1929-30)
> Andrew Redan Rogers (1929-34)
> Guy William Neal
> Brian Winslow Thynne and
> Douglas George Wragg.

Cricket XI, 1941
Top row, from left to right: C. Lucas, ?, J.D. Mawson,
D. Kilgovv; Middle row: Colin Morgan, J.D. Link, G. Edwards,
J.W. Jenkins and P.E. Richardson who later played for England.
Seated on the mat are twins J.W. Warley and G.T. Warley

England XI for the Second Test V West Indies, 1957
Back Row: P.E. Richardson, F.S. Trueman, R. Tattershall,
T.W. Graveney, D.B. Close, D.V. Smith, M.C. Cowdrey
Front row: J.B. Statham, T.G. Evans, P.B.H. May, T.E. Bailey,
J.H. Wardle

Those that returned and took tea with Miss Gamlen and Miss Phillips were to learn that the wind of change was blowing towards the Cathedral Prep School.

Evidently the Governors (Dean and Chapter) of the Cathedral School and Headmaster C.F. Scott (since 1940) wished to relinquish responsibility for the Prep School, where it was rumoured discipline was causing concern. It is easy to forget that esteemed headmistresses like Miss Dance and Miss Gamlen were employed by and subject to the Governors and Headmaster of the Cathedral School—and in 1947 they put the Cathedral Prep School on the market.

CHAPTER 6

The
Independent Gentleman

The new owner was Robert Thomas, Housemaster of the Junior Boarding House at Bedford School, who, prompted by his desire for a career change, an attack of jaundice and a welcome legacy, arrived in Hereford in 1947 to 'look at' the Prep School. He was accompanied by his mother-in-law. His wife Nora who remained in Bedford with their young family recalls the enthusiasm of the two on their return because 'ancient cathedral cities appealed to both of them'. A further inducement was the fact that he knew the new Headmaster of the Cathedral School, Jack Hopewell, whose former school, Victoria College, had been evacuated from Jersey to Bedford where a friendship developed with the Thomases. Nora Thomas, previously School Matron then Housemaster's wife, was also delighted at the prospect of becoming the Headmaster's wife of a day Prep school with no Saturday school and looked forward to a more leisurely existence.

The family duly moved from Bedford to take up residence in the flat above the school. Four year old Hugh Thomas relished having a school playground for a garden which at that stage had not been surfaced with tarmac.

'There were no classrooms at the lower level, which had been a rifle range at one stage. I remember spending hours digging lead out of the timbers at one end of the range. There was no classroom in the main playground area, but there was a large bench against the wall and beneath a huge beech tree which grew in the Steele's garden next door and had to be lopped from time to time to provide us with a view from the flat over the Castle Green nurseries [now Redcliffe Garden] to the Wye and the Bishop's Meadows beyond.

'The classrooms for forms 1 and 2 must have been built soon after we arrived because that is when I began my school life at the age of five. Rather than simply walking across the playground and down the steps to my classroom, I wanted to be like everyone else and so I would go to and from school by walking along Castle Street and then down Quay Street and into school through the green door in the brick wall which now had a new sign "Cathedral Preparatory School".'

Hugh's first form teacher was Miss Ford and his classmates were Roderick Thomas, Roger Court, William Steele, Roger Millichap, Neville Eckley, Graham Smith, Timothy West, Christopher Edge, Robert Davis, Bobby Morris and Jimmy Thorne. The last, now a civil engineer, writes from Bogra, Bangladesh, of his prep school experiences, recalling visits to his friend Hugh's home, 'a flat which, when I ventured into it, had all the trappings of what I thought of as luxury.'

The arrival of the Thomases in Castle Street was an event: after a string of unmarried headmistresses, the Prep School had a family man for Headmaster.

'We've got a Headmaster,' one small boy proudly told his parents on seeing Mr Thomas at morning assembly in his gown, 'and he wears a black mackintosh!'

Warmed by the welcome, Robert Thomas nevertheless knew there were serious issues to confront. He must restore public confidence in the reputation of the Prep where he had been told 'the discipline was appaling'.

He knew he must enforce discipline and must be seen to do so. Shortly after his arrival, his own form misbehaved so he 'slippered' the whole class. It was a make or break situation. Various parents objected but all except one accepted the Headmaster's ruling. The remaining parent, who exerted considerable influence locally, arrived on the Thomas's doorstep on a Sunday morning to

Miss Phillips and Headmaster Robert Thomas from the 1948 school photograph

have his complaint dismissed by a courteous but firm Mr Thomas with the words, 'I would not expect to do business with you on Sunday so I bid you good morning.'

Suffice it to say the Sunday visitor's sons all completed their education with distinction after this confrontational start.

Discipline was established and rules kept to a minimum in what so many staff and pupils of this era have described as 'such a happy school.'

Inevitably, however, the shame of a 'slippering' was something few boys forgot. Jim Thorne (1948-54) who was in Miss Ford's class with his friends Roderick and Hugh Thomas (not relations) remembers every detail of his most traumatic early school experience concerning a newly built wall, 'due to the mixture of shame, mortification and an early sense of injustice which it left me with.'

'The wall which was about 18 inches high and finished with a curved cement mortar topping with a greenish tinge, was built one summer holiday to identify the end of the playground and to stop urchins running onto the two metre wide rose bed which separated the wall from the precipitous drop to the lower level.

'The wall was an ideal height for sitting on, and that was what I was doing one break when I saw a carefully carved little hole in the new mortar, undoubtedly made by one of the numerous penknives which little boys of the era could not be without. As luck would have it, one of my larger marbles fitted wonderfully well into the hole and I spent a few minutes of harmless enjoyment putting it in and fishing it out again. I was aware of a prefect not far from me during this activity, who later reported me to Mr Thomas for having created the hole.

'In Mr Thomas's study I was subjected to the most intense inquisition. Did I dig the hole? "No, Sir", "But X saw you." etc. continued for some minutes until I was babbling incoherently under the cold eye of Mr Thomas that I did not even own a penknife—which was certainly being economical with the truth, but I was too far gone in fear and apprehension of the terrible injustice being done to me to worry about how I was going to get out of this scrape. "I shall beat you, not for having made the hole in the wall, but for having lied about it." Oh, terrible ignominy, as the fateful canvas shoe is produced and I receive six of the best, peeing in my pants and weeping with shame and humiliation.'

Mr Thomas's 'special slipper' (a tennis shoe) replaced Miss Gamlen's cane on the hand. It was administered in the Headmaster's study which he called his 'beehive', after which miscreants learnt to 'beehive' themselves was how he put it!

It must be said that the vast majority of pupils passed through the school without sampling this experience, though all were quick to relish the discomfort of those who did! Nigel Heins (1950s) remembers the rush to the classroom wall adjoining the study to count how many whacks the offending boy received.

'I remember one boy returning to class, saying it had not hurt at all because his wallet was in his back pocket. He was very rich so it was probably true!'

Christopher Mann (1948-53) has not told his parents to this day about the slippering he received when he missed afternoon school to play with his new little spaniel puppy.

On another occasion Christopher was summoned to the study after class only to discover that Mr Thomas had 'decided for some reason to teach me Latin and without any explanation began with the declension of the Latin "to love". He said he would test me the next day and I remember repeating over and over again on the way home: "Amo amas amat, amamus amatis amant".'

The ordeal seemed pointless until recently when, as an ancient-history documentary film maker, he found himself filming on the top of Nimrut Dag, one of the highest mountains in Turkey. 'There King Antiocus had had his epitaph carved—and later that year I found myself looking at tiny remnants of an ancient plaque in a Saharan oasis. In both cases, the ideas in the minds of the writers became clear by studying the tell-tale tenses and cases of these small clues from antiquity.'

Mr Thomas taught both Latin and French, the latter with what he jokingly called his 'Parisian' accent. His methods were unorthodox but very effective. Inevitably in such an academic environment the less able occasionally found life less pleasant. The P.F.W. (Positively Final Warning) and subjection to the 3 Weekly Report (a child on this report had to have a card signed by the teacher at the end of every lesson with comments on his work) followed misbehaviour and/or poor school work. 'A bit of extra help would have been far preferable', comments Michael Carr (1960s). One favourite method of testing involved the Glow Worms and Slow Worms: an early form of setting. Mr Thomas's son Hugh admits to 'probably being a Slow Worm' but found his year with 'Sir' very amusing. 'I think we were only there for his own amusement—the fact that we were being taught at the same time was almost a side issue.' Certainly Mr Thomas loved teaching and in later years was frustrated by the administrative paperwork which limited his time in the classroom.

A general knowledge test was turned into a game called 'Whizzing Up and Down' when the pupils left their desks and formed an orderly queue in the classroom. Those who got the answer right moved up the line as many places as the number of those previously asked the same question had failed to answer it. This very competitive system was, as Jim Thorne (1948-54) puts it, 'very appropriate for the day and completely discredited a generation later, when a newer, softer approach had it that only harm could befall the academically-challenged in such win or lose competitions.' It certainly boosted the confidence of some, like the little boy who went home and told his mother he was a genius after one such competition.

In 1952-3, a sudden fit of patriotism (probably induced by the Coronation) got to Mr Thomas when he introduced 'houses' called by the name of one of the Regimental Guards: Grenadier, Hussar, Fusilier, Coldstream etc. (This was before the subsequent Headmaster, Keith Hill, named the Prep School houses after the four who lost their lives in the Great War.) Each boy endeavoured to collect stars for good performance for his own house/regiment. Those who distinguished themselves were personally congratulated by Mr Thomas in the 'Beehive'. Nigel Heins remembers 'the joy of being made Captain of Grenadier House—only for the [House] tournament to be cancelled because of waterlogged pitches. We would have thrashed the Fusiliers out of sight.'

Fierce competition achieved excellent results enabling boys to go on to the Boys' High School, Cathedral School or other boarding Prep schools which would prepare them for Common Entrance to Public Schools at the age of thirteen.

Numbers increased significantly, so in 1954, to accommodate extra pupils in No.28, the Thomases moved out of their flat to a private house. New classrooms were also built, one in the immediate playground and the other on the lower level below. There was no shortage of new pupils to fill them so Mr Thomas had clearly got his sums right!

Nora Thomas tells how her husband found Maths difficult at school and this made him realise how his pupils would feel if they didn't understand and were unable to keep asking questions. Tables printed on the back covers of exercise books were learnt by heart, starting with the two times table. Like so many others, Film Director Chris Mann still uses his multiplication tables nearly half a century later. 'They have never let me down when a calculator is not at hand or an instant decision is needed during a phone call.'

An abiding memory of a History lesson also remains. 'The swing between Catholicism and Protestantism in the early seventeenth century was graphically represented to us by us all drawing in our exercise books a giant pendulum swinging backwards and forwards. On the left side it was blue and the right pink. Ten years ago I was making a Songs of Praise in Lewes in Sussex about religious intolerance and terrible burnings at the stake. And lo and behold that wonderful helpful image sprang up from my subconscious and there it was, just the image to bring the times into focus.'

Some efforts were also made to introduce the rudiments of watercolour painting in a room above the canteen from where a staircase led to it and nowhere else. From the school dining room in the immediate post-war period emanated smells of over-boiled cabbage which with mushy peas and spam followed by puddings soaked in custard were prepared by allegedly grumpy ladies in the adjacent kitchen.

Mr Thomas with his form in 1962
which included his daughter Julia (the first girl at the Prep),
here seen sitting beside her father

School meals obviously improved. By 1965, David (known by his initials as D.E.N.B. Jones), the then new young man on the teaching staff, admits to enjoying the extra large portions with which he was favoured. He lists the staff he joined that September, starting with the Infants' Department: Mrs Higham, Mrs Evans, Mrs Cullis, Miss Hurst and Miss Woods. Mrs Gray also joined the staff during the ensuing three years and Mrs Barrett, who replaced Miss Lewis as School Secretary, writes from Portugal to congratulate the school on its centenary and wonders whether any of the pupils who helped with the First-aid box went on to become doctors.

David (1965-8) records his one claim to fame: the introduction of a school library of some 500 books borrowed from the Schools' Library Service and renewed each term.

'Mr Thomas was a little worried by this at first, especially when I told him it was a free service. "What will the parents say, David, when they know it is a free service? After all, they're paying fees and we're getting something for nothing. It's hardly right—it's like receiving charity," were his sincere comments. My advice to him was not to tell the parents! I wonder if he did! But we had our library and everybody was pleased—including the parents!'

According to Shirley Hurst (1959-66), another young teacher, the parents were extremely co-operative. 'They were free to come and see us if they wished, but on the whole they trusted the staff and let us get on with the teaching. I do not remember any Parents' Days at all.'

What Shirley does remember—all too clearly—is 7th January 1959, the day she came for her interview for her post of assistant mistress at the Prep.

'It was cold with slushy snow falling. There was chaos in the heart of the city with traffic (even then!) Mr Thomas met me at the railway station, took me to Castle Street, showed me round, interviewed me, took me to lunch in Hafod Road with his wife and youngest child and offered me the job!

'I presented myself on the first day of the summer term—28th April. I was young and nervous and knocked timidly at the front door. This was opened by a young woman (Deborah Thomas) who told me politely but firmly that I ought to have come in through a side door. I was taken up some back stairs, worn, unstained and battered by many small feet, into a classroom on the first floor. The sight that met my eyes filled me with utter horror—masses of small boys in short-trousered grey flannel suits running along the top of desks. Panic! What had I done? I took a deep breath and ordered them to get down. To my astonishment, they obeyed. So I began seven happy years at the Prep.

'Mr Thomas, a man of complete integrity, spoilt me for all future heads. He told me at interview that he would never interfere and he never did. He seemed to have complete confidence in all his staff.'

This impression of Mr Thomas is endorsed by all his former staff to whom I have spoken or written. Throughout his 26 years as Headmaster, he was regarded as the perfect gentleman by all staff and parents without exception. Certainly the impression I received on introducing my son Paul to his new Headmaster in 1970 was of an ageing, distinguished, cultured gentleman who spoke with authority but without pretension.

Jennifer Higham (1959-98) remembers him as a 'true gentleman' who wrote her a letter every summer holiday thanking her for her year's work.

His gentlemanly conduct occasionally raised some smiles. David Jones describes one such incident:

'One morning, after assembly, he asked all the ladies to retire to the staff room as he had something to say to the boys that was a little delicate. He then addressed the boys, telling them that he was rather disgusted that one, or more, had thought fit to put a toilet roll down the lavatory, and declared that it should never happen again. He was too much of a gentleman to mention 'lavatory' or 'toilet roll' in the presence of the ladies! This was the sole incident in my ten terms which caused Mr Thomas to be angry and to feel that he had to reprimand the whole school.'

Good manners also prevented Mr Thomas from telling a teacher who took games that it was inappropriate to do so clutching her handbag!

Games no longer took place on the Cathedral School playing fields at Wyeside. The Prep School's independent status deprived it of the right to such a facility. While the younger pupils played games on the Bishop's Meadow, 'chocolate-coloured' coaches with metal floors transported the older ones from Castle Street to the City Sports' Ground in Grandstand Road twice a week. Shirley Hurst, Hilary Alcock and Deborah Thomas (the Headmaster's daughter who acted as secretary 1958-9) shared the chilling experience of taking Football there. 'At this,' says Hilary, 'I was totally useless and always chose a keen player to direct the refereeing.' Shirley adds, 'It used to seem like the wastes of Siberia in winter, but the weather had to be really bad for it to be cancelled. Mr Thomas put great emphasis on the importance of games.'

At Sports' Day, also held in Grandstand Road, enthusiasm ran high. Deborah and her mother won't forget the chore of getting all the prizes together. Mrs Thomas remembers they decided to discontinue the Fathers' and Sons' Race 'because Doctor Gordon Wilson said he saw stars when he was running and we thought we might have a fatality.'

Deborah also recalls joining in swimming lessons at the Edgar Street Baths, when her father (immaculate even in swimming trunks) paced the length of the baths with the long pole from which a webbing strap extended round her waist as she floundered in the water.

Evidently the Headmaster's daughters caused quite a stir amongst the boys! Julia was the first girl pupil (September 1961-July 62) who declares 'I was there at the instigation of my father, the Headmaster. He wanted me to get a grounding in French, Latin and Maths or rather Algebra and Geometry, all subjects he taught. I certainly had little option but to concentrate hard as he made me sit in the front, facing his desk, where those famous bushy eyebrows were often raised, keeping an eye on my work.'

John Hardwicke (1957) remembers all the boys (once out of sight of the Headmaster's study) clustering round his daughter 'like bees round a honeypot'!

The years passed with the daily crush into the dark hall for the simple act of worship at morning assembly with boys on stairs and in doorways, the annual search for a willing virgin for the Christmas play and the ever so gradual increase in school fees which Mr Thomas was reluctant to increase even by 10 shillings (50p) a year.

Robert Thomas was nearing retirement. He wanted the Dean and Chapter (who comprised with a few others the Governors of the Cathedral School) to buy back the Prep School. They showed no interest. Their priority was the financial stability of the Cathedral School itself (threatened by the withdrawal of the Direct Grant) which they ensured in 1973 by their decision to admit girls.

Finally—after a considerable time—Robert Thomas sold his school, not to the Cathedral School but to a member of its staff, who was himself an old boy of the Prep: Keith Hill.

CHAPTER 7

The Dorstone Experience

Keith Hill entered the Prep School in 1940, the same year as C.F. Scott became Headmaster of the Cathedral School. 'We'll be new boys together', that august figure had told Keith's parents. Their son was to use similar comforting words to new pupils when, 33 years later, he became Headmaster of the Prep. Bill Quan (74-77) recalls how 'the Headmaster in assembly informed us that if we were nervous—not to worry—he was too and it was also his first day in the job.'

In 1973 when the Prep was for sale, Keith was teaching at the Cathedral School, a place he knew well. He had been educated there, returning after 5 years 'away' for National Service in Egypt and 3 at Cambridge, at the request of the Headmaster Jack Hopewell to act as House tutor in the Deanery. Later he was to become a Housemaster. His associations with the Prep school included long standing friendships with Miss Gamlen and Miss Phillips.

After her engagement to Keith, Judy Hill remembers him taking her to see Miss Gamlen, who was then very old and living on Aylestone Hill.

'She took us to her cupboard and said, "Choose something, dear, for a wedding present." I didn't know what to have. Eventually I chose 6 plates. I've still got them.'

In 1973 Miss Phillips wrote to Keith from Hampton House Residential Home.

'I am so very pleased you are taking over the Preparatory School and I wish you and your wife every success in the future. I feel so happy in the thought that the School is in the hands of an "Old Prep" who knows all its history and traditions and I hope your rule as Headmaster may be long and very happy. I was very happy indeed in my thirty-eight years there.'

As for the Prep School itself, the only sight Keith had had of it since leaving as a boy was 'when Robert Thomas hung flags out not only for the Coronation but, in true independent fashion, for his wife's return from hospital.'

Judy remembers the day Keith came home and said, 'The Prep's for sale!' They were both convinced that if they didn't take the chance and buy the school, they would regret it later although 'on a schoolmaster's and physiotherapist's salary, we weren't going to find it easy to raise the money.

'We sold our home and some possessions and managed to borrow some money and moved into the top floor of the school.'

The Prep had been going through a difficult transition period. People were wondering if the school was going to continue. Jennifer Higham remembers teaching an Infant class of only seven, a reflection of parental concern over the future of the school.

The new Headmaster had some adjustments to make. 'Little' boys were a different breed to the 11-18 year olds he had been used to teaching at the Cathedral School. His wife recalls 'When we were moving in, some of them came up and commented on our possessions, Keith was amazed.' He was not even allowed to get near his youngest pupils. Jennifer Higham had given him strict orders, 'You're not to come and talk to them because you'll make them cry.'

A more serious disappointment awaited Keith. When he inquired about joining the Independent Association of Preparatory Schools, the prestigious association of prep school headmasters, he was told that the Hereford Cathedral Prep was far too closely connected with the Cathedral School to be accepted. 'And so we were—in every way except financially. We hung on for years and years but it wasn't until we got boys into Marlborough and Winchester that I.A.P.S. were glad to welcome us—in 1986.'

Keith and Judy were not deterred by this initial set back. With a respectable set of letters after their names (Keith Hill was not only a Master of Arts but also an Associate of the Royal College Of Music; Judy Hill, Member of the Royal Society of Physiotherapists became a Justice of the Peace in 1978). They were determined as Judy's mother put it 'to run a proper prep school', (though difficult without boarders), in which boys would be prepared for Common Entrance to Public Schools at 13—even if they were going against the national trend in pursuing a policy which closed other 'proper' prep schools. In retaining some pupils for a further two years, they were therefore seen to be reducing the intake at age eleven to the Cathedral School. (At this time Belmont Abbey didn't take boys till 13, though as numbers dropped, along with practically every other public school they reduced their intake age from 13 to 11).

The introduction of the Common Entrance syllabus sharpened and widened the academic approach at the Prep. Keith Hill comments, 'A Winchester entry paper would make your hair curl in the sheer breadth and depth of knowledge required.' Between 1974 and 1987, in addition to 159 out of 184 passing into the Cathedral school at 11, 5 out of 5 into Brecon and 11 out of 13 into Monmouth, of the 131 who took Common Entrance, 123 passed at the first attempt. 4 retook and passed so only 4 out of 131 failed altogether. During this period a wide range of schools received boys from Hereford Cathedral's Prep: Bedstone, Belmont, Dean Close, Duke of York R.M.S., Dover, Downside, H.C.S., Loughborough College, Marlborough, Monmouth, Old Swinford Hospital, Oundle, Shrewsbury, Woodhouse Grove, Worcester Royal Grammar, Winchester and Uppingham.

'Man with a mission' is how Bill Quan (74-77) describes Mr Hill. Looking back, Bill realises how things improved during his three years at the Prep. In 1974, he came 'as a raw country boy' from a primary school with a school swimming pool and gym where he had enjoyed excellent school dinners.

'My first day in Castle Street was a shock to the system—no swimming pool, no gym, a very cramped playground and school meals that even for my unsophisticated palate and considerable appetite were a struggle to consume.

'Within a year many reforms were introduced such as P.E. in the Cathedral School Gym, swimming lessons at the City Baths, while classrooms had that much needed lick of paint and the food improved.'

On his own admission, Bill was 'no great achiever academically ... but it has to be said that I have much to be grateful to the Prep for. They got me into the Cathedral school. I played my first game of rugby in about '75 with amongst others Phil Morgan, Allan Parker and David Blandford, all of whom I still play with at Luctonians some 20 years later.'

Bill is one of many who benefited from the all round education offered at the Prep which included the very special Dorstone experience involving two afternoons a week devoted to 'outdoor' activities.

'We were looking for an extra dimension,' said Keith, 'and so we bought 12 acres at the Bage, Dorstone, where little boys could ride, camp, fly-fish, row and canoe in safe water (as far as any water is safe).'

They also bought what Keith describes as 'a steel, tug-type diesel motor boat named *Brabo* (after the strong Belgian dwarf),' in which they took boys along the Severn, and through Holland, Belgium and France over the years. 'It is typical of my wife's support in all matters,' Keith comments wryly, 'that when we came to take the Royal Yacht Association navigation exams, she passed, I failed!'

Judy, an experienced horsewoman offered riding tuition which conveniently could take place in all weathers in one of the massive barns at the Bage, scene of popular dressage demonstrations where rosettes pinned to the wall whisper still of past triumphs. Christina Bodger (now Shaw) was employed to teach stable management on a weekly basis. Riding lessons also took place at Fawley where a pupil's grandparents opened their farm to the school. The interest thus fostered led to participation by Prep School pupils in the I.S.I.S. Junior Riding Competitions at Moffatts School near Bewdley, a practice which has continued for 21 years, with three former pupils becoming successful race jockeys.

Another activity which could be pursued in all weathers at the Bage was archery, for which one of the barns was suitably equipped. Andrew Dobson (1981-86) recalls going to Dorstone

54

The Dorstone Experience

every Saturday and particularly enjoying the archery. (Saturday was an opportunity for choristers and boarders to enjoy the facilities— and any other members of the School who wished, at extra charge.)

Archery was supervised by Bill Anderson, Prep school teacher turned professional sports' instructor.

When it came to designing the half-acre assault course, the expertise of the S.A.S. was called upon. John Pace (ex S.A.S.) both designed and ran the course. Race tracks were also well received by B.M.X. enthusiasts.

These were the years of the Dorstone summer camps. Happy memories of 'camping in an army tent in a field and washing ourselves and our cutlery in a stream.'

More typically, curricular sports took place in various locations in Hereford: cricket, rugger and soccer at the City Sports' Club and athletics on the Hereford Athletics' Ground. Optional extras existed like badminton in the H.C.S. gym and squash at the Whitecross Squash Club.

'Everyone always looked forward to the House matches,' declares Andrew Dobson who played rugby and captained the cricket team. His headmaster had created a new House System, choosing a set of four new names: the four old boys who had died in the First World War: the Boys' Own Heroes of Chapter 2. Worthy names to perpetuate. Scoring the winning goal for Matthews against Woodhall is something Andrew Dobson won't forget.

Nor will he forget his first play, 'Witches and Bananas'. 'I was most upset at having to be a witch and dress up as a woman. I had set my heart on being a banana. Basically the play consisted of us running around the stage of the Nell Gwynne theatre on broomsticks. The next play was "Joseph and the Multi-coloured Dream Coat". At first I was cast as the king, then I became the butler. Finally I was cast as the baker who was only in one scene because the king had him beheaded. So much for my acting career!'

Nevertheless Jennifer Higham remembers six year old Andrew giving a spectacular performance parading round the Cathedral as a wise man. Other productions were 'Sweeney Todd', 'Scenes from the Life of Schubert' and mini operas performed at the Garrick Theatre in imitation of the Vienna Boys' Choir.

Pupils were creative and fulfilled on the stage, the assault course and in the class room. Good results silenced critics who thought that time spent travelling to and from and at Dorstone meant less emphasis on the academic aspect.

Scenes from 'A day in the Life of Schubert' with William Gibbon as Schubert (seated at table, wearing wig, glasses and beige jacket)

57

'There were always plenty of takers for Dorstone,' Jennifer Higham told me. 'Even a waiting list, I believe, first come, first served—so obviously parents thought it worthwhile. The clientele changed in this period—with more moneyed parents entering their sons.'

Discipline was maintained, corporal punishment now more a threat than a reality. Andrew Dobson sums it up with the following tale:

'We were caught melting crisp packets on a heater to make them shrink. We were told to go and see Mr Hill at break time. All the other boys were petrified that they would get the cane, but as I was new I did not believe that we would get caned for such an innocent act. We were not caned but each given a stern ticking off, it would be the cane next time. This threat worked and no one in my class ever got the cane while I was at the Prep.

'The usual punishment given out by teachers was to be sent out, this happened to me on many occasions.'

Punishment was probably more of a talking point amongst pupils than a cause for concern. An incident that did cause concern however was the appearance of some noisy and disruptive youths on the Castle Green. Terrified pupils were reassured by the immediate action taken by the Deputy Head, John McQuillan, a Classics M.A. from Aberdeen, but with a background from the slums of Glasgow. John took two of the offending youths by the throat, and with the other men on the staff, dragged them into the Infant Department where they were 'persuaded' to wait for the Police.

Such concerted action and the fact that there was no rapid turnover of staff also speaks for itself. 'Of the original ten teaching staff, six (including two Heads of Department) were still there when I retired,' comments Keith Hill. His last staff meeting was held on the Eiffel Tower in Paris—as a thank you.

He presented the School with a silver cup for the Headmaster's Essay Prize. In his own words, 'Academically I nailed my colours, so to speak, to the English Essay. I had worked my way up the Cambridge marking system to being on the revising board. I suppose, with leading teams and personal marking, I had been responsible for about 40,000 essays, so I knew what an essay should be.'

Cathedral Preparatory School Staff in 1987
From left to right: Mrs J. Stafford, Mrs J. Higham,
Mr. J. McQuillan, Mrs S. Talbot, Mr R. Hall, Mrs A.F. Davis,
Mr. C.W.M. Anderson, Mrs. A. Rhodes, Mr. M. Antcliff,
Mrs P. Lewis, Mr S. Jarvis, Mrs H. Roberts and Mrs J. Wictome,
with Keith and Judy Hill (seated)

Ironically the first winner of the Headmaster's English Essay Prize was Chinese!

As he approached retirement, Keith Hill's wish, like that of his predecessor Robert Thomas, was to see the Cathedral Prep become once again part of the Cathedral School. The time had come to sell. Several years elapsed before the Dean and Chapter made a move. They were aware that whereas there were 160 on the School roll in 1973, numbers had fallen to 109 by 1987. Negotiations eventually resulted, therefore, in their offering to buy the goodwill and rent the building from the Hills for 7 years. Eventually—in 1994—they bought the freehold. They were not, however interested in perpetuating the Dorstone experience. Keith and Judy were very disappointed; they had looked forward to continuing their link with the School from their home at Bage Pool.

Disappointment was mitigated by satisfaction in seeing the Prep returned to its *alma mater* which would ensure its survival for the foreseeable future.

CHAPTER 8

Two in One

In 1987 the Senior School was completely co-educational, while the Junior School educated boys only. With the appointment of a new headmaster by the same governors who served both schools, this was bound to change.

They appointed Stephen Sides, the Director of Music at Prestfelde in Shrewsbury. His first sight of 28 Castle Street was hardly encouraging: 'After modern buildings and rolling acres of Prestfelde, to come to a Georgian town house with no space in the centre of a city was a daunting experience and initially very off-putting. It was snowing hard and bitterly cold. Both Janet and I came for interview the following week—it was snowing again and still bitterly cold, but the interviewing panels and all the governors were so welcoming that we realised when we were offered the job that we would be well-supported and befriended—and so it was to be.'

Cathedral Organist and Choirmaster Dr Roy Massey recalls his own satisfaction with the appointment of a practising school musician as Headmaster who acted as his own Director of Music in the Junior School.

'He knew all about producing boys' voices from his own experience and sat in on the Choir Voice Trials. When you listened to his school singing, they weren't ordinary breathy little voices. He knew how to produce a voice and as the years went by, the quality of singing improved. When a boy came from the Junior School as a chorister, his voice was already being formed because Stephen

Dr Roy Massey, M.B.E., Cathedral Organist and Choirmaster conducting a voice trial for the cathedral choir with the support of Headmaster Stephen Sides in the background.
(Jeffery G. Wilkinson)

knew how to do it which was a great bonus and of course he was very sympathetic to the pressures of choir boys because he knew all about them.'

During the next eight years Hereford Cathedral Junior School emerged from the chrysalis of the Prep. The transformation involved adjustment and some heartbreak. Jennifer Higham recalls 'tragic redundancies, nasty shadows on the School's history.'

The Junior School stretched its wings to include all the Senior School facilities which became formally available, including the lawn and dining room of No.1 Castle Street where Speech Day and barbecue lunches took place. For their Advent and Christmas Carol Services the School was now entitled to use the Cathedral. Stephen remembers too 'the tremendous sense of partnership and camaraderie which developed with the Senior School music and drama departments during the rehearsals and performances of annual concerts and shows including "Bugsy Malone", "Brilliant the Dinosaur" and "Helen come Home".'

The Senior School maintenance team turned their attention to the Junior School. Out went the cream and chocolate paintwork and gas fires in the classrooms. Technology arrived to the relief of Sue Press, the School Secretary. Stephen describes how 'in order to make a phone call, I had to contact Mrs Press by a series of buzzes on the phone. One buzz meant: I want an outside line, two meant pick up the phone, and three meant, I can't remember—probably, "Come and rescue me from this difficult parent!" If Mrs Press wasn't in the office, I had to run down to answer the phone or to put the line through.' But by 1995 the new fibre optic system had arrived giving instant access to any part of the school site.

Numbers increased. In 1987, there were 109 pupils with a few in the Nursery. In 1995 the School had 223 pupils with 38 in the Nursery. By 1995 boys had accepted girls in class as the norm. The first eight had joined H.C.J.S. in 1990: Isobel Sides, Alice Berry, Ruth Dickson, Sarah White, Lisa Cheng, Jessica Lambert, Adele Cullum and Joanne Alderton. Ruth and Isobel had already been in the school for over a year since they had both started in the Nursery. Of the two, Ruth enjoys the distinction of being the first girl to go right through H.C.J.S., leaving in 1997 to join the Senior School. She describes her impression of those early days:

'I didn't think the school was that scary at first because my older brother was still in the same playground as me.'

She expected to wear a cap similar to his. 'So I had already made plans to wear his cap when he had grown out of it.' Instead she had to come to terms with 'itchy tights' and 'feeling a bit small in assembly'. But there were compensations like 'at birthdays when the teachers let you blow out the candles on a fake cake

The first girls on arrival in 1990 and on leaving in 1997.
From left to right: Isobel Sides (not in 2nd photo), Alice Berry,
Ruth Dickson, Sarah White (not in 2nd photo), Lisa Cheng,
Jessica Lambert, Adele Cullum and Joanne Alderton.
(Courtesy of Hereford Times*)*

made out of a Rose's tin.' Unfortunately though, on Ruth's birthday, the cake had broken!

Like most boys of a similar age, Peter Griffiths (1991-95) took the girls in his stride, recalling instead the fun of being a dinner monitor 'and also the drawback of cleaning up the gravy and yoghurt after the little ones.' Then there was the reward of a jelly baby when Mr Wells signed his prep book at the end of the week!

Jelly babies might be restricted but everything else was on the increase: numbers on the school roll, games' fixtures, scholarships and the school site. With girls and boys spilling out of 28 Castle Street, expansion of the school site was essential. The way forward was to use premises occupied by the Senior School which could in turn expand elsewhere.

Meanwhile the Junior and Senior School were building on their new relationship. Things became a little strained when a special staff meeting of both was called to discuss not only the development of the former but also whether it was now necessary to have two headmasters of what appeared (to the public anyway) to be one school. A unanimous desire to preserve H.C.J.S. as a separate entity with its own headmaster was evident.

The undisputed growth of H.C.J.S. was also acknowledged and in due course it was agreed that the Senior School should vacate No.29 Castle Street in favour of H.C.J.S.

No.29 is rated as a two star listed building. Only 2% of listed buildings in England are Grade 1. In Hereford these include the Wye Bridge, the Cathedral and the Old House. The next 4.1% are two star, No.29 rating with the Conservative Club and Farmers' Club in Widemarsh Street as a very important building.

Historically its interest lies in its rear wing which embodies the late 14th century hall of the original College of the Vicars Choral. These priests were required to sing seven daily services in the Cathedral during the late Middle Ages. Aware that negotiating the unlit muddy path to the Cathedral subjected these singing vicars to muggers, Bishop Stanbury and Earl Ferrers arranged for cloisters to be built next to the Cathedral. Thus the Vicars Choral were provided with a safe and dry corridor connecting their quad to the Cathedral and in 1473 left Castle Street for the Cloisters.

Many years ago a floor was inserted in the Vicars Choral hall, but the original roof timbers that provided the ceiling are still visible in No.29 in what is now an upstairs flat, providing attractive accommodation for teaching staff.

Appropriately it was under Stephen Sides, whose empathy for the choral tradition was well known, that arrangements were made for H.C.J.S. to occupy 29 Castle Street.

Stephen himself was preparing to move on, to become Headmaster of St. Paul's Choir School, but there are some things he will never forget about his time in Hereford. He recollects 'The Christmas Carol service, with tableaux done by pre-prep, when during the choir's singing of "Silent Night", Mary and Joseph started a hay fight across the crib, burying baby Jesus in moun-

Headmaster Tim Lowe. (Tony Bolton)

tains of loose straw, an angel wetting himself and a shepherd falling asleep, waking up suddenly and howling for his mother.' And 'Evensong on a wet November evening when just the lights in the choir stalls are on and the rest of the Cathedral is lost in shadows.'

With the departure of Stephen in July 1995, the running of the school was left in the capable hands of Bob Hall, Acting Headmaster until January 1996 when Tim and Karen Lowe arrived. Previously Deputy Head of Wells Cathedral Junior School and Marketing Officer for both Junior and Senior Schools at Wells, Tim is clearly well equipped to take H.C.J.S. into the next century, an affable manner accompanying the breath of fresh air which he brings to the job.

'The benefactor of the growth of the school' is how he describes himself. With two teenage daughters, Emily and Harriet, and his eleven year old son Matthew, he is essentially a family man for a family school which has educated sons of local families through the generations and is now welcoming their daughters. H.C.J.S. has become fully co-educational. Numbers have escalated to 275 with 30 in the Nursery housed in the cheerful homely atmosphere of No.2 Castle Street, which feeds the Junior School which in turn feeds the Senior. It is likely that in future H.C.J.S. will provide half the intake into the latter. The Junior and Senior schools are both established as two separate schools under one governing body, with the autonomy of the Junior School clearly preserved.

In addition to St. David's Hall which is used for daily assembly, plays and concerts, the school now occupies three adjoining buildings linked by two courtyards. No.30 Castle Street, formerly the School Bursary was taken over by H.C.J.S. in September 1997 and has become a specialist teaching area for Years 3-6. All classes restrict their numbers to 16. The I.T. Centre at No.30 supplies each child with an individual P.C.

'Information Technology is their future' says Tim Lowe as he confronts the task of taking H.C.J.S. into its next century, but he will not do it alone for that is not his style. His first two Speech Days indicate a new approach. No more stifled yawns during the Headmaster's speech! In July 1996, he persuaded the staff choir

Information Technology Centre in 30 Castle Street. (Tony Bolton)

known as 'the Barber's Shop' to amuse parents with their rendition of 'In the Jungle'. 'The staff have a great sense of fun,' he says. 'It's nice for parents to see them in a different light. You need something in Speech Day that's light-hearted!'

In July 1997, Kate Harrison, B.B.C. Education Correspondent for the Midlands, was the guest so Tim talked about prop cards used for broadcasting, producing some children's prop cards which his pupils illustrated by appearing in sports' kit, with musical instruments, or dressed as teachers, choristers etc as props to his speech.

'Each year you want to be different,' declares Tim—an exciting prospect for Centenary Year and beyond!

CHAPTER 9

Laudate Dominum

A school history is essentially a history of its pupils and teachers. Each one plays his or her part. The inclusion of the 1997-8 school roll and list of staff, many of whom have given long and dedicated service speaks for itself. There remain a few whose service or achievements deserve a special place in the school's history, whether individually or as members of teams and to these representatives I give the last words.

'An institution' is how many refer to Jennifer Higham. A childhood friend of Deborah Thomas, she came to the Prep straight from school to help with secretarial duties in 1959. A few months later, the Reception Class teacher left unexpectedly. Jennifer found herself in charge of her first class of five year olds under the supervision of Mrs Edwards, who with others on the staff, recognised her potential and persuaded her to go and train. Thus in Autumn 1961, Jennifer, now married, embarked on a three year Teacher Training course at Hereford, the youngest married student that they had had. In due course a letter arrived from Robert Thomas offering her the opportunity of applying for the vacancy that had occurred in the Infant Department. So began a career which included a parachute jump for charity and outlasted three headmasters.

Much has changed. Jennifer recalls a two and a quarter hour lunch hour in Mr Thomas's day, 'now there's not a minute to breathe.' Discipline is 'different', gone are slipperings and cane but Jennifer commands the same respect as she always did.

Jennifer Higham with Charlie Davies and Annabelle Dent.
(Tony Bolton)

Much has changed certainly but Jennifer remains extraordinarily patient and solicitous for the four year olds in her care, taking them, for example, on an annual visit to the County Hospital to allay fears, while the names and circumstances of the hundreds who have passed through her hands are rarely forgotten.

One such is John Hardwicke (1957-61) who remembers Jennifer as a young teacher and admits to a schoolboy crush on her. 'When she got married I was determined to give her a wedding present. With my two and six [12 pence] pocket money I bought six teacups in the Cattle Market. I couldn't afford the saucers but I was so proud because I had bought them with my own money.'

I have personal reason to be grateful for the mine of information that is Jennifer Higham. It was she who reminded me to include 'Scu'.

Peter Scudamore, the most successful jump jockey of all time, is probably the most famous old boy of the Prep to date. His partnership with Martin Pipe, begun in 1986, smashed all National Hunt records providing him with the ammunition to become champion every year until his retirement at 34 in 1993.

D.E.N.B. Jones (1965-8) remembers 'only too well how Peter would endeavour to bring a horse into nearly every essay. I mentioned this on one occasion to his father, Michael Scudamore, who rode to victory on *Oxo* in the Grand National in 1959. I asked Michael if his

Peter Scudamore jumping the last fence in front in the Sun Alliance Novice Chase at Cheltenham on Young Hustler

son was going to be as good a jockey as his father, to which Michael replied, "Better!" As a boy of 10, Peter Scudamore made a remarkable prophecy in one essay I set entitled: Myself in 10-20 years' time. Peter wrote something like this: "I am now nearly 30, and I have been Champion Jockey for the past 3 years." This prophecy was mentioned by his father when Peter appeared on "This Is Your Life".'

The finest cricketer that the Prep ever produced is Peter Richardson (1936-41) whose brother Derek, known as Dick (1940-42), also played once for England. In 34 tests, Peter scored 2,000 runs for England, including a remarkable 104 in the Laker Test against Australia at Old Trafford in 1956—at an average of 37.47. He appears in the photograph of the Prep's Cricket XI in 1941 with twin brothers George and John Warley.

Cricket continues a popular sport at H.C.J.S. Since 1977, Bob Hall has coached the School under elevens, members of his teams winning the Hereford Primary Schools' Cup in 1986-9, 1992, and 1994-5, while the Rugby Sevens also distinguished themselves in the Bluecoat School Sevens' Tournament of 1994 and 1996. This success in rugby was maintained when H.C.J.S. became Hereford Invitation Sevens Champions in 1996, also winning the Hereford Schools' Rugby Tournament for under elevens in 1997. The Hereford Primary Swimming Champions for 1995 also hailed from the Junior School, not forgetting of course the County Champions in chess in 1993 and 1995.

Robert Hall with cricketers Binul Shah, Philip Burbery-Wills,
Oliver Powell and James Sweetman in the new Sports' Hall
in the Zimmerman Building. (Tony Bolton)

The girls made history in 1996 by playing their first Hockey and
Netball matches, as did the first Lacrosse team consisting of boys and
girls who became West Midlands under eleven champions in 1997.

Pupils were no doubt inspired by the example of Justin
Pugsley, their Head of English, who had represented Great Britain
in the World Cross-Country Championship in Italy in 1996.

1997 also saw the Junior School Choir performing in the
National Festival of Music for Youth in the Queen Elizabeth Hall,
Southbank, London, while the Cathedral choristers toured Ireland.

The presence of choristers at H.C.J.S. dates from 1976. Dr Roy
Massey explains how and why choristers appeared in the Prep two
decades ago.

Choristers on the oak staircase in 28 Castle Street, Christmas 1987. From left to right: Timothy Sarson, Richard Brown, Dominic Willsher, Marc Silverthorn, Christopher Powell, Ceri Brown and Alastair Macdonald

'When I first came in 1974, boys came into the Choir only at age eleven when they started at the Cathedral School. Presumably the picture since time immemorial. That's very late for a choir boy to start, resulting in a pretty quick turnover as the average voice goes at 13 or 14.'

In 1898 when the Prep School was founded, Choirmaster and Organist Dr Sinclair had boys singing at 15 or 16 and was even well known for obtaining apprenticeships for his choristers who, when they left the choir, went to work.

Dr Massey was confronted with a very different situation. He had not only to contend with choristers who had a short choral life of two to three years, but his arrival in Hereford coincided with the Cathedral School's decision to go independent. This followed the withdrawal of the Direct Grant in 1973, which had guaranteed choristers a totally free education up to the age of 18. The responsibility for funding the choristers now fell on the Dean and Chapter who came up with a scheme for paying two thirds of a chorister's school fees. They also summoned Dr Massey to a Chapter Meeting and asked him two questions: How did he see the future of the choristers? What would he like to happen regarding them?

Dr Massey replied that it had always worried him that he didn't get his choristers until age 11. 'Couldn't we link up with the Prep school?' he asked. 'Start them at eight rather than eleven?'

Fortunately Keith Hill, the Headmaster at that time, was sympathetic to this idea and young choristers have been educated at H.C.J.S. ever since.

'The ramifications of this,' adds Dr Massey, 'were if they were boarders, they would have to board in the Junior Boarding House where at that time the youngest children were eleven. Children coming in at the age of eight would completely change the character of the Junior Boarding House which in accordance with the wise advice of the Headmaster of the Cathedral School, Barry Sutton, would need to include at least two boarders coming in at that tender age.'

Subsequently Junior Boarding Housemaster, Egerton Parker, generously agreed to accept eight year old Paul Hartley and John Padley as boarders. They were very good singers who got the scheme of younger boys off to a very good start. In future a little boy who passed the voice trial and transferred to the Prep School at the age of eight had also the option of boarding if he lived too far away to meet his strenuous obligations in the Cathedral.

Paul Hartley came from York. Dr Massey's abiding memory of this 'delightful independent little fellow' concerned the first choir practice of term usually on a Saturday evening, meaning choristers came back on Saturday evening to practice, sing on Sunday and start school on Monday.

'Paul was always late because of his train. We knew he'd get there eventually. The door of the Song School would open and a very large fishing rod would come in, followed at some distance by a very small boy. He was a very keen fisherman, so he always brought his fishing rod back with him and rather than take it straight to the boarding house, he used to bring it to Choir Practice.'

The Bishop owns the fishing rights of the stretch of river fronted by the precincts of the Cathedral and the Bishop's Palace, so Paul got permission from his friend Bishop John Eastaugh to fish from his garden. Dr Massey describes how 'on Sunday he would belt out after morning service and with the aid of a forked twig set up his fishing line on the river bank, return to the Cathedral to sing Evensong and be out of the vestry like a shot after the service to see what he'd caught.'

As for John Padley, equally independent and 'very bright', he followed in his choirmaster's footsteps by becoming an organist and after playing for a year at St. George's Cathedral in Jerusalem, became assistant organist at Sherborne Abbey.

Since the days of John and Paul, the number of choristers in the Junior school has increased. In October 1997, 8 out of 18 of the Cathedral choristers came from the Junior School.

New staff are introduced to the demands of a chorister's lifestyle by an invitation to join the Dean and Headmaster of the Junior School at a sung Evensong in the Cathedral. After sitting together in the choir to listen to the singing, they walk across to the Deanery for refreshments and the opportunity to talk about the pressures and professionalism of a chorister's life.

The Very Reverend Robert Willis, who became Chairman of the Governors of Hereford Cathedral School (both Senior and Junior) in 1993, stresses that today singing is only a small part of what the school represents—that out of 800 odd pupils spread throughout the Junior and Senior schools, there are only 18 choristers. The Junior School do not, like the Senior, worship daily in the Cathedral, although they use it regularly for occasions like Harvest Thanksgiving and carol services. However since 1987, the Junior School has been part of the human family foundation of the Cathedral which includes the Chapter, the choristers, both Senior and Junior Cathedral schools, the Library, Song School and domestic buildings. Pupils of the Junior School can't help being aware of the Cathedral's life with choristers coming in and out of lessons and chatting about their routine. The Dean's badge on every blazer underlines the ongoing link with the Cathedral.

School Chaplain Father Geoffrey Howell reads to pupils in the Medieval Room in 29 Castle Street. (Tony Bolton)

In 1994, Father Andrew Hutchinson was appointed as school chaplain to H.C.J.S. His job combined the personal care of the choristers with that of Succentor of Hereford Cathedral and as such formed another bridge between school and cathedral. In 1997, he was succeeded by Father Geoffrey Howell who lives in No.3 Castle Street next to Tim Lowe, the Headmaster of the Junior School at No.4. 'A nice juxtaposition', comments the Dean, 'for the Head-master and the Chaplain are both responsible for the pastoral care and the way in which the Christian faith is presented to the members of the Junior School.'

As Chairman of the Governors, the Dean is aware of the way H.C.J.S., 'a very strong section of the Cathedral School', has grown and developed since 1993.'It has its own ethos. It can relate to other schools connected to cathedrals which have the same ethos. An ethos which it didn't have as a Prep school, because then it wasn't a Cathedral School.'

It is now linked to the Cathedral, to the continuity of worship and education through the centuries which has served the community through the ages. The Dean and Chapter value 'the presence of all these young children in our midst and the sense of education going on in a modern and developing way.' Hereford Cathedral Junior School has its own very important part to play in the Cathedral's life as it embarks upon its second century. As the Dean puts it, 'A Cathedral can become so high and mighty. It needs to test its integrity and faith against children's questions because it's always the child who will shout, "The Emperor has no clothes!"'

Floreat Schola Minor Herefordensis.

Staff on 1st January 1998

	Date of Joining	*Responsibilities*
Headmaster		
Mr T.R. Lowe	1996	
Deputy Head		
Mr R.I. Hall	1977	Science, Cricket, Chess
Mrs E.A.A. Ashford	1989	
Mrs L.M. Bandtock	1997	
Mr T. Brown	1991	History/Geography, Rugby
Mrs A. Dale	1993	Special Needs
Miss K.A. Davies	1997	
Mrs A.F. Davis	1986	
Mrs E.M. Dickson	(HCS)	Design Technology
Mr N.M. Eggington	1994	Housemaster, IT
Mrs F. Field	1995	Art
Mrs P. Gammage	1995	
Mr D. Grace	1988	Maths, PE, Football
Mrs J. Higham	1959-61, 1964-66, 1971	
Revd G. Howell	1997	RE
Miss N. Jeynes	1997	
Mrs K.E. Lowe	1997	Registrar
Mrs P. Lewis	1972-74, 1979	French, Swimming
Mrs D.J. Parry	1993	Infant Music, P.S.E.
Mr J.A. Pugsley	1995	English, Drama
Mrs E.A. Rhodes	1979	
Mrs H.M. Roberts	1974	
Miss R.H. Shepherd	1996	Music
Mrs S.V. Talbot	1978	
Mrs B. Walker	1991	Head of Nursery
Mrs R. Walker	1996	Girls' games
Mrs M.J. Wictome	1978	
Mr R.A. Wintle	1998	Director of Studies

Non-teaching staff

Mrs M. Eggington	1994	Housemother
Miss H. Gittens	1996	Assistant Matron
Mrs B. Griffiths	1980	Ancillary
Mrs F. Harding	1997	Ancillary
Mrs J. Jenkins	1984	Domestic
Mr M. Lowe	1997	Gap Student
Mr A. Rushdi	1989	Caretaker
Miss E. Williams	1997	Gap Student

Administration

Mrs S. Press	1986	Headmaster's Secretary
Mr F.D. Langstaff	1986	Bursar
Mrs M. Barnacle	1987	Assistant Bursar

Junior School & Nursery Roll, January 1998

Aftalion, Jason
Aftalion, Marc
Agate, Luke
Agate, Matthew
Ainscough, Evie
Ainscough, Thomas
Ainscough, Hannah
Allman, David
Allman, Thomas
Anscomb, James
Asprou, Michael
Attwater-Davey, Edward
Baggott, Robbie
Bagley, Joel
Bagley, Leah
Bailey, Charles
Bailey, Lucy
Ball, Katherine
Ball, Joanna
Bamber, Joshua
Bamber, Michael
Bann-Murray, Lonan
Barazetti-Scott, Jared
Barazetti-Scott, Joshua
Barling, Daniel
Barnes, Matthew
Barnett, Nicholas
Barrow, Thomas
Barton, Jonathan
Barton, Thomas
Bates, Olivia
Beavan, Tom
Bellew, Joshua
Bemand, Jonathan
Bennett, Thomas
Berry, William
Berry Ottaway, Charles
Bevan, Tom
Bird, Charles

Bird, Harry
Blake, Patrick
Bowler, Charlotte
Bowler, John
Boyd, Ellen
Bradley, Ben
Brain, Jamie
Brain, Lara
Breeze, Timothy
Broadbent-Jones, Elliot
Broadbent-Jones, Henry
Brown, Alexandra
Bullock, Jessica
Bulmer, Charles
Bulmer, Jeremy
Burbery-Wills, Philip
Burdett, Emily
Burns, Alex
Butler, Oliver
Campion, Thomas
Carr, William
Cass, William
Challenger, John
Chambers, Joanna
Chase, James
Clay, Molly
Clay, Wil
Cohn, Hugo
Collings, Charlotte
Collings, Frank
Collings, Harriet
Connop, Sarah
Corbin, Callum
Corbin, Jamie
Corder, Ian
Corder, Megan
Corder, Michael
Cook, Gillian
Cotterell, Richard

Coughtrie, Emily
Croke, William
Cross, Luke
Cross, Oliver
Cullum, Oliver
Cumberlidge, Rebecca
David, Tessa
Davidson, Becky
Davidson, Georgina
Davies, Carrie
Davies, Charles
Davies, Edward
Davies, Helen
Davies, Isabella
Davies, James
Davies, Kimberley
Davies, Lisa-Jane
Davies, Oliver
Davies, Spencer
Demaus, Antony
Dent, Annabelle
Dickson, Angus
Don, Freya
Don, Thomas
Dowling, James
Duggan, Iain
Eakins, Nathalie
Edgar, Oliver
Edwards, Genevieve
Erskine, Robert
Evans, Howell
Evans, Lloyd
Evans, Rachel
Eynon, George
Fisher, Joseph
Fisher, Luke
Ford, Elliott
Ford, Jordan
Fox, Luke
Furness, Peter
Gammage, Bethany

Gardner, Alice
George, Isobel
George, Simon
Godwin, James
Goode, Edward-James
Gray, Alexander
Gray, Sophie
Gwyther, Edward
Gwyther, Harriet
Harbord, Benjamin
Harding, Claire
Healey, Beth
Hensby, David
Hensby, Harriet
Higman, Rosalind
Hill, Faye
Hiscox, Lewis
Hobby, David
Hobby, Emma
Holt, Matthew
Hunter Choat, Felicity
Hunter Choat, Sarah
James, Polly
Jeffery, Richard
Jennings, William
Jinman, Henry
Johnson, Toby
Jones, Ashton
Jones, Boe
Jones, Christie
Jones, Matthew
Kaye, David
Keating, Patrick
Kedward, Lauren
Kempe, Katherine
Kempe, Sara
Kent, Christopher
Kenward-Gibbs, Katie
Kimber, Daniel
Kimber, Richard
Kippax, Benjamin

Kippax, William
Knight, Jeremy
Knight, Jonathan
Knight, Rosannagh
Knight, Thomas
Lalor, Miles
Lambert, William
Leccia, Joshua
Leccia, Olivia
Lee, Ailsa
Lee, Eleanor
Leech, Felix
Leech, Frances
Leeds, Kimberley
Leeds, Nicholas
Leeds, Richard
Lewis, Benjamin
Lewis, Hugo
Lewis, Joe
Leysham-James, William
Lifely, David
Lifely, Freddie
Lifely, Thomas
Lowe, Siân
Lowe, William
Mackay, Laura
Main, Alastair
Main, Andrew
Mainwaring, James
Majeed, Nadia
Marshall, Thomas
May, William
Mercer, Charles
Meredith, Richard
Middleton, Carita
Middleton, James
Mifflin, Edward
Mifflin, James
Mills, Katherine
Morgan, Polly
Morris, Jack

Moyle, James
Moyle, William
Nash, Edward
Nenadich, Nicola
Nenadich, Christopher
Nowosielski, James
Oliver, Edward
Orgee, Joe
Page, Edmund
Pantall, Harry
Pantall, Jack
Parker, Duncan
Parkes, Oliver
Parr, Alasdair
Peberdy, Russell
Pember, Mason
Phillips, Charlotte
Phillips, Harry
Phillips, Louisa
Pincombe, Matthew
Pincombe, Thomas
Powell, Michael
Powell, Oliver
Powell, Robert
Price, Benjamin
Price, Charles
Price, Joseph
Pring, Andrew
Putland, Otto
Ramage-Smith, Benjamin
Ramage-Smith, Samuel
Rawlinson, Felix
Rawlinson, Sam
Rawlinson, Zoë
Rawstorne, Angus
Rees, Alexander
Reid, Hannah
Reid, Martin
Robertson, Anna
Rumney, David
Rumney, Fiona

Sargeant, Edward
Scully, Maxwell
Shah, Binul
Shirazi, Ben
Shirazi, Rebecca
Sibly, Olivia
Slater, Alexandra
Sleath, Henry
Sleath, Oliver
Smith, Miles
Smith, Nicholas
Smith, Sebastian
Sole, Julian
Sole, Philippa
Spearing, Rhodri
Spearing, Thomas
Spicer, William
Stafford, John
Stanbridge, Chloe
Stanbridge, Daniel
Steele, Eleanor
Stinton, Freya
Stoddard, Duncan
Stoddard, Lara
Stoddard, Natasha
Stokes, Andrew
Stones, Charlotte
Struthers, Mark
Surrey, James
Sweetman, James
Tabernacle, Nicholas
Tatchell, George
Tatchell, Kate
Tatchell, Martin
Taylor, David

Taylor, Jack
Terry, John
Tingley, Graham
Tompkins, Emily
Tompkins, James
Tompkins, Matthew
Vakatalai, Naomi
Valentine, Jack
Valentini, Alexander
Wall, Camilla
Wall, Jessica
Wallis, Peter
Warner, Emily
Warner, William
Warwick-Jones, Murray
Watkins, George
Watkins, Julie
Watkins, Richard
Webb, Georgina
Wesley, Elizabeth
Whitcombe, Madeleine
White, Charles
White, Natalie
Wilding, Olivia
Williams, Abigail
Williams, Christian
Williams, Claudia
Williams, Robert
Williams, Russell
Williams, Virginia
Wilson, Richard
Wikser, Annabel
Wisker, James
Young, Richard

Index

Edge, Christopher 42
Edwards, G. *39*
    Mrs 69
Ellesmere College 16
Emerson, Miss 36
Evans, Mrs 47

Fawley 54
Ferrers, Earl 65
Fisher, Patrick R.C. 38
Ford, Miss 42, 43
Francis, Ronald 32
Fusilier House 45

Gamlen, Miss 17-22, *21*, 23, 25,
    26, 28, 29, 30, 32, 33, 36,
    38, 40, 51
Gaza War Cemetery 16
Gibbon, William 57
Glennie, Minor Canon 6
Gray, Mrs 47
Grenadier House 45
Griffiths, Peter 65

Hall, Robert *59*, 67, 71, *72*
Hardwicke, John 50, 70
Harley Court 1, 2
Hartley, Paul 74
Head, Lt Cmdr Clement 12
Heins, Nigel 44, 45-6
Henson, Mr 6
Higham, Mrs Jennifer 47, 49, 52,
    56, 58, *59*, 62, 69, *70*
Hill, Judy 51, 53, *59*
    Keith 33, 51-60, *59*, 74
Hinks, John Hawksford 38
H.M.S. Dolphin 11
    Maidstone 12
Hopewell, Jack 41, 51
'Houses' 45, 56
Howell, Father Geoffrey 76, *76*

Humby, C. *27*
Hurst, Miss Shirley 47, 48, 49
Hutchinson, Father Andrew 76

James, Alwyn David 38
James, Roger Hereford 38
Jameson, Lt Cmdr A.G. 11, *12*
    J.W. *39*
Jarvis, Mr S. *59*
Jones, Christopher Averay 38
    D.E.N.B. 47, 49, 70

Kempe, Katherine *24*
Kilgovv, D. *39*

Lambert, Jessica 63, *64*
Lewis, Miss 47
    Mrs P. *59*
Lincoln, Mistresses 1
Link, J.D. *39*
Lowe, Karen 67
    Tim *66*, 67-8
Lucas, C. *39*

Macdonald, Alastair *73*
Mann, Christopher 44, 46
Marriott, Max 17
Martin, Miss 28
Massey, Dr Roy 61, *62*, 72, 73,
    74, 75
Matthews, Capt John Bredel
    15-6
    John 22, 28
Mawson, J.D. *39*
Millichap, Roger 42
McQuillan, Mr J. 58, *59*
Morgan, Colin *39*
    Phil 54
Morris, Bobby 42

Nimrut Dag 44

West Heath School, Hampstead
    16
West, Timothy 42
Weston, Anthony 36, 37
White, Sarah 63, 64
Wictome, Mrs J. 59
Williams, B. 27
Willis, Very Rev Robert 75
Willsher, Dominic 73

Wilson, Dr Gordon 49
    Mrs M.E. 26
Woodhall, Lt John 15, 16
Woods, Miss 47
Wordsworth, J.C. 28
Wragg, Douglas George 38
Wyeside 28, 49

Ypres 15